OUR American STORY

RICK & KARA GREEN

Our American Story

© 2009 by Rick and Kara Green.

For additional copies of this book or for more information on other books by Rick Green, contact:

Rick and Kara Green
P.O. Box 900
Dripping Springs, TX 78620
(512) 858-4825
www.rickgreen.com

Cover design & photography by Callie Shepherd
www.callieshepherd.com

Printed in the United States of America

ISBN   9780976935469

To Our Parents:

Richard & Pat Green

and

Terry & Nelda Kyle

We want to thank you for setting a Godly example and laying the foundation for us to raise our kids in the nurture and admonition of the Lord.

OUR AMERICAN STORY

Contents

OUR AMERICAN STORY

Dear Reader,

When we travel as a family and speak all across America, we are often asked questions about many aspects of our lives – from our first run for political office, to how we homeschool and travel at the same time, to how we attempt to keep a balanced life with many projects going on simultaneously.

This book is our attempt to give you a glimpse into the last 15 years of many ups and downs in the Green Family, but most importantly, share with you the many wonderful memories and blessings along the way.

We will also share with you why we have a passion for educating and inspiring Americans across the nation about our Godly Heritage and why we feel it is so important to pass that knowledge on to our youth so they can be equipped to win the culture war for many generations to come.

However, what we want to convey the most is that our family is not special. There is nothing we do that cannot be duplicated and taught by many others. In fact, there is nothing new under the sun and most of our strategies were learned from other American families like David & Cheryl Barton, Dickie & Charlotte Halbgewachs,

Paul & Billie Kay Tsika, and so many other great role models.

We believe it is imperative that more Christians become educated about the intent of our forefathers and teach the truth to their families, starting with their children. As Americans, we should all feel the burden of preserving the precious liberty that has been paid for with much blood and sacrifice. We must do all we can to make sure that our children enjoy the same freedoms we have today.

*We hope at the end of this book, you have laughed and been inspired, but most importantly, we hope you believe that **you and your family can make a difference!***

By His Grace,

Rick and Kara Green

PART I
A FAMILY PURPOSE

A good name is rather to be chosen
than great riches, and loving favour
rather than silver and gold.

Proverbs 22:1

OUR AMERICAN STORY

1

Rick

What does it mean to be a part of the Green Family?

Well, it depends upon who you ask.

If you ask our close family and friends, their answer would most likely be…*"CHAOTIC!"*

Kara and I would say…*"joyful, eventful, and meaningful."* We certainly have our highs and lows, our embarrassing moments, our shortcomings, and our strengths. Our prayer is that somehow we take all those strengths and weaknesses and do our best to make our lives count for something.

Top row: Reagan, Rick, Trey / Bottom row: Kamryn, Kara, Rhett

Most importantly, we want them to count for God's Kingdom…in whatever way He chooses to use us.

As a part of that Kingdom purpose, we pray our lives will be spent making our local church, community, state, and nation better places than they would have been without us.

A few years ago, Kara, the kids and I decided that if we're going to make a difference, we needed our own family mission statement.

I have a hard time saying *"no"* when people ask me to be part of a project. I would speak everywhere I was asked and take every opportunity I was given...but God gave us 24 hours in a day and no more.

So a mission statement allows us to consider every opportunity and every invitation and ask the question, *"Does this opportunity fit within our mission and purpose?"*

We took some time putting the mission statement together because we wanted to make sure that it included the whole family and covered every area of our lives within what God has called us to do.

The next page is a picture of how the framed Family Mission hangs in our home.

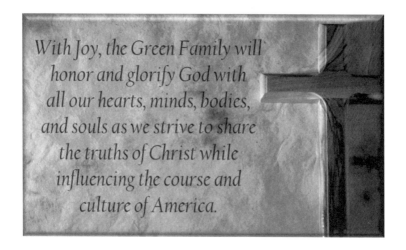

With Joy, the Green Family will honor and glorify God with all our hearts, minds, bodies, and souls as we strive to share the truths of Christ while influencing the course and culture of America.

WITH JOY

The first two words of our mission statement really set the tone for everything else..."*with joy.*"

Have you ever noticed how much easier it is to do a tough task if you do it with joy? That does not mean you have to be "happy" with the circumstance or process because happiness and joy are two different things.

As I recently heard on a CD of Paul Tsika, II, joy comes from *within* as a result of our relationship with Christ, so it does not come or go based on external circumstances. Happiness, on the other hand, is a response to those external circumstances we are pleased to be experiencing at the time.

One can be very *un*happy with what is happening to them, but have joy while working hard to change the circumstances.

For instance, I am very unhappy with the current state of political affairs in America as leftist officials are attempting to transform our nation into a socialist state. But the decisions of our Congress do not control my joy. Whether or not my favorite candidate wins an election does not control my level of joy.

Rhett & Kamryn

Whether or not my boys win a baseball game I'm coaching does not control my joy, though it may impact my happiness for that particular moment.

The Green family *attempts* to approach everything in our lives *"with joy."* I say *attempts* because a mission statement is not a magic wand. We often fall short of the mark, but we don't lower the bar or give up trying just because we have days in which we forgot the joy of our salvation.

The joy of our salvation has a powerful impact on our attitude and actions because we recognize that our salvation or our position in Christ does not change with the seasons, government actions, or individual mistakes and victories.

So whether we are playing a baseball game, speaking in front of thousands, making a long haul drive back home in the bus, cleaning the house, cutting brush, stuffing envelopes, doing our Bible Study, or washing the dog...we try to remind each other to keep the joy of our salvation front and center.

Kamryn helping the family clean up our property by
picking up sticks and brush....not her favorite activity,
but she pitched in with the rest of us and kept her joy!

We recently studied the life of Joseph in our
family devotional.

Wait a second.

Before I go any further, I want to make sure you
are not conjuring up a picture of the perfect family
gathered around the breakfast table with Bibles
opened next to eggs, bacon, toast and orange juice
with all the children sitting perfectly still and quiet as
their father takes the family through a complete and
thorough study of the entire Bible and then imagining
that we do that every morning like clockwork.

In our dreams!

Or maybe on the many "lists" Kara will talk about later. Reality turns out very different for us most of the time.

We want to be very honest and real with this book, not purposefully creating any perceptions different from our reality. The truth is that we strive to do the best that we can, but consistency in schedule is just simply not our strong suit. We almost never have two

Dad trying to keep from being pelted with confetti filled eggs

days in a row with the same schedule, so we just have to honestly say that a regular morning family devotion is not a reality in our life.

We do attempt to have breakfast and devotion together as often as possible, but it is never as often as we would like. So we encourage the kids to study on their own in addition to our group devotions, and we constantly look for opportunities throughout the day to apply God's Word to the situation at hand. Now, back to Joseph…

This was a guy that kept his joy in the most disturbing of circumstances. He was sold into slavery by his own brothers and later put in prison for a crime he did not commit. Yet in every circumstance, he kept his joy and asked God to use him wherever he was at the time. I believe his attitude of gratitude in even unsavory and unfair situations is why God continued to elevate him until he was second only to Pharaoh, and God used him to literally save the world from starvation.

So now when one of the kids (or one of us parents!) appears to be without joy, then another member of the family will simply ask, *"Are you in prison? Have you been sold into slavery?"* So far, that has been enough to jolt the

Rhett

less than joyful person back to reality and fulfilling their mission *"with joy."* The best response yet came from six year old Rhett when asked if he understood what it meant to be sold into slavery. He said, *"Sure, it's like being sold on ebay."*

HONOR & GLORIFY GOD

"Will Honor & Glorify God..." is a pretty broad umbrella, but the idea is to make sure the focus is on God and not on ourselves. When our mission or goals are only about what we can personally do, be, or have, just for the purpose of doing, being, or having, we become self-centered and ego-driven.

When the ultimate mark is that everything we do is for His Glory and to honor Him, it is much easier to do things His way and get the focus off of ourselves.

This mission also has a built in system of accountability. No matter the circumstances or the task, we can always stop and ask ourselves if we're engaged in an activity that is honoring and glorifying

God and also ask whether or not our performance within the activity is bringing honor and glory to Him.

George Washington is one of our favorite role models.

WITH ALL OF OUR HEARTS, MINDS, BODIES, & SOULS

If we are to honor and glorify God with all of our hearts, minds, bodies, and souls, then we must give our best in everything we do and we must use all that God gave us.

All of our heart means with passion and love, grit and determination, perseverance and patience.

All of our mind means studying hard, being as prepared as possible, and using the brain God gave us and not shying away from any intellectual issue or discussion. If we feel inadequate on issues like evolution, or philosophy, or history, there has never been an easier time to dig deep and learn about any subject in the world for very little, if any, expense.

With just a few clicks of the computer, one can begin to get a cursory knowledge about virtually anything. The volume of Christian authors and experts is amazing. You can find a DVD, CD series, or book on any topic. That way you can choose the learning method that best works for you...visual or auditory. There is no excuse for letting our minds waste away or for not knowing about the issues of our day.

All of our body means taking care of the temple the Lord has given us. We are not health nuts and we do not do nearly as much as we should to take care of our bodies, but this is one area the Green family is working hard to do better. The bottom line is that the healthier you are, the more energy you have, and the more you can physically do every day to fulfill your purpose.

Trey focused on giving his best

All of our souls means that we endeavor to grow spiritually. As the apostle Paul said, bodily exercise profits little, but godliness is profitable in all things. This area of our mission is met through personal and group devotion, public worship, and feeding our souls with good books and CDs teaching us how to better serve the Lord.

SHARING THE TRUTHS OF CHRIST

Every time we spread the Good News, whether to one person or ten thousand, we fulfill this part of the family mission. The Good News includes not only the news of eternal salvation through Christ, but also the earthly salvation that comes through the practical benefits of doing things His way. These benefits apply across the board to individuals, families, businesses, schools, communities, states, and nations. This is how being salt and light makes a difference in the culture.

INFLUENCING THE COURSE AND CULTURE OF AMERICA

Those benefits are laid out extremely well in David Barton's aptly titled book, *The Practical Benefits of Christianity*. This concept explains the motivation behind everything our family does to influence the culture through politics, education, media, the pulpit, business, etc.

Our goal is to implement the very same policies the Founding Fathers drew from the Bible for the very same reasons they did...because it makes for the most free, most Blessed, most prosperous nation possible.

When we move away from doing things God's way, we get the same lackluster or even horrific

Reagan, Rhett, Trey, & Kamryn at the Creation Museum

results that any other nation has experienced when they rejected God.

So our family has dedicated itself to influencing the world around us as best we can...that is our calling. We fulfill that calling through public speaking engagements, radio programs, authoring books, serving in public office, and speaking up for truth every chance we get.

If we're on top of our game, then we are doing all of that *with joy* and we're using every bit of our hearts, minds, bodies, and souls to accomplish the task. If we're having one of those days where it seems like we're missing the mark, then hopefully one of the younger ones will pipe up with, *"Are we in prison? Have we been sold into slavery? Alright then, let's get some joy back and get on with the mission!"*

WHAT IS YOUR FAMILY PURPOSE?

You and your family have a mission and a purpose to fulfill as well. Maybe you already know what it is and you are working with joy to fulfill it.

Maybe you've never even thought about it, but your heart has been searching for more purpose.

You don't have to travel the nation or speak to thousands of people to impact the world around you. No two families I know have the exact same mission and purpose.

The important thing is that you find YOUR family's purpose, write a mission statement to define it, and then set about fulfilling it.

Your family may only consist of you right now, or it may be an average sized homeschool family of 27 under one roof ☺.

You might be 18 or 80 or somewhere in between. No matter your age or your circumstance, God has a purpose for you to fulfill.

No one else can tell you exactly what that purpose is. Others can help breath a little destiny into you by pointing out some of your strengths or by highlighting particular areas where God is Blessing you with favor, but only you will know for sure when you hit the sweet spot…His Perfect Will for your life.

Our purpose in writing this book is to encourage you to find and fulfill your family's purpose. We pray that our stories will make you laugh and maybe even give you some ideas of things that you, too, would like to do. Most of all, we pray that you start taking action today on whatever assignment the Lord has given you!

The foundation of national morality must be laid in private families....

John Adams, Diary, June 2, 1778

OUR AMERICAN STORY

★

2

Kara

We first made the decision to homeschool when our oldest son, Trey, was five and we had to make a decision about what to do for kindergarten. Thinking back, I can remember how I just could not imagine letting this little guy, whom I

loved to be with every day, spend so many hours away from Rick and me only to be more influenced by his peers at school than his mom and dad at home. He just seemed so young to send away every day for that many hours.

I honestly do not remember having that "moment" where I just knew we had to homeschool, but I had always been open to it. My mom had homeschooled my youngest sister for a couple of her high school years. Rick had also been homeschooled during some of his younger years, so we were both very comfortable with the idea of homeschooling.

For us, making the decision to homeschool was not an agonizing one that took a long time to make. We knew in our heart this was the best solution for us as a family. We love a new challenge. Even though we had a 5 year old, a 2  year old, a 9 month old, and Rick was serving in the

Texas Legislature, we were 100% committed and have never regretted our decision.

Now that our kids are older, we travel a lot and homeschooling still works best for us. We are now in our 8th year, and all 4 of our kiddos are officially being homeschooled.

SCHEDULE SMEDULE

One thing I am asked about a lot is whether we keep a rigid school schedule.

Well, let me just say for the record, the answer is NO!

Let me also say that you do not have to keep a rigid schedule where your whole day is planned out in 30 minute increments in order to be a successful homeschool family!

Every family is different.

Therefore, every family has to come to a conclusion about what works best for them. I have some friends who do like to have a schedule and that works out great for their family.

I will admit that in the past, at the beginning of the school year when I am really motivated, I have valiantly tried to print out a pretty schedule with all the kid's activities for the day and what pages they should work on in each school book. That lasted for maybe a week and then real life set in and the schedule went out the window.

This does not mean that our home is in utter chaos. We do have order, regular chores, and a long "to do" list every day. I am big on LISTS! I love my lists, and my post it notes. It's not un- heard of for me to even stick a post it note on myself somewhere so I don't forget what I'm supposed to do!

When I first started homeschooling Trey, I had a pretty simple schedule, but as we had more kids I had to re-arrange the schedule every school year to accommodate the changes in our lives. This is still true today. When every school year comes around, our life has changed in some way from the previous year, so no two school years are the same.

SCHEDULE WRECKER

We are very blessed to have Rick work from home. When we are not traveling, the kids have the freedom to visit with Rick in his office any time of the day, and Rick very often will emerge from his office (usually right in the middle of school!) and announce, *"Everyone get out your bat and glove...let's go play some ball!"*

Well, in record time all four kids jump up, run out the front door, and leave me in their tracks sitting at an empty table with their school books everywhere, wondering when we will get school finished that day! Hence, that's why a rigid schedule does not work for us! With all of the little interruptions that we encounter throughout the day, you have to be flexible.

Another reason for our very unusual schedule is that Rick and I have always been night owls. I get my second wind at night and will often get more done after 10:00 PM than I will the rest of the day. It is not uncommon for me to be dusting, vacuuming, and doing laundry late into the night. We just are not "wired" to be morning people.

Our kids have adapted to our schedule, which means that if any part of their school was not finished during the day, we use this opportunity at night to finish it. We have never been the type to get up at 7:00 AM *(Rick says that hour of the morning is only good for two things – hunting or sleeping!),* start school by 9:00 AM, and be finished promptly by 3:00 PM. If you are homeschooling your kids and feel the pressure to conform to a certain way of doing things, please do not put that pressure on yourself.

My personality is to have order, cleanliness, be able to see results, and keep a zillion different lists. I like to have a place for everything and I can hardly focus on anything else until my kitchen is clean! I do not naturally like change and am very happy being a home body. So, the one trait I have been forced to adopt is flexibility. In order to homeschool with joy, you have to be flexible.

Rick's personality is to be the visionary, be spontaneous, and live in the moment. He has a type A (or type triple A as I like to call it) personality. Everything he does, he does it 1000%. What that means is that we always have more projects than we can physically handle at one time. Rick and I  always work together on our political and business ventures, so balancing school and Rick's projects is always a challenge, but at the end of the day, I would never change the lifestyle we have.

KEEPING THE PURPOSE IN MIND

I naturally have those days where I feel like I am just spinning my wheels, or I start wondering whether I am cheating my kids out of a "better" education from a private or public school, but God is so good. Through all of the little things that I get to enjoy with my kids, He reminds me daily why we homeschool.

I have been able to witness spiritual growth in all of them, have the most meaningful heart to heart conversations, and create so many precious memories with each one of them for which I will always be so grateful. Ultimately, the most important job  we have in homeschooling and parenting is to raise our children with a desire to serve the Lord.

I am far from being an expert homeschool mom. In fact, I rely so much on the advice and direction of many other homeschool moms who have been doing this much longer than I have. Every day is a learning experience for our whole family. What I have learned over the last 8 years is that you have to be willing to adjust your schedule to accommodate the changing seasons of your life; you have to be flexible and learn to be spontaneous, and most importantly, approach each day you have with your kids with joy…..even if the kitchen isn't clean!

**Kamryn getting help from Daisy with
her schoolwork outside**

HOMESCHOOLING ON THE ROAD

Even though homeschooling on the road might sound difficult, believe it or not, it is actually quite easy. You see, I can get distracted easily when I am at home. For instance, as I'm walking to our school room to answer a question for one of the kids, I'll see that pile of clothes on my bed that has been sitting there for 2 days needing to be folded. I'll think to myself, *"I'll just spend 5 minutes folding and get it started, then I'll come back and finish it later."* Well, during that quick 5 minutes, my kids have either lost their train of thought with their schoolwork and they are now walking around the kitchen looking for a snack, or they are looking at me saying, *"Mom, where have you been? I really need your help."*

Rick and I also run our business out of our home, and there are always emails to answer back, phone calls to return, endless errands to run and so on. So, that is why I say it is easy to homeschool in our bus. I don't have all of the distractions that I do at home. Our phone is not ringing, there are no dishes sitting in the sink, and I don't have a washing machine to be constantly washing laundry in. I am forced to focus on the kids and their school. I often find that our time on trips is when I get to spend more time reading to the kids and spending one on one time talking and having some wonderful conversations. We will often take several good books that we all enjoy and while Rick is driving, we will all sit at the front of the bus and read the book out loud together.

We spend a lot of time in our studies talking about our American Heritage and what it means to be an American. We want to prepare our kids to be able to defend their belief in God and their love for their Country. Those are two areas where we can't afford to fall short. I am asked quite often about our history curriculum and what we use to teach our kids their memorization on the Declaration.

We use A Beka Books curriculum for all of our courses, but we also supplement with many different things for history. To be honest, it is hard to say exactly how we study history. We read biographies on the founding fathers, we read their speeches, and Rick and I are always reading a new political/historical book for ourselves.

Many times we end up sitting around the table at dinner talking with the kids about what we learned through our reading. Many times, the most impactful learning comes when we are in the car driving. Just the other day, Rhett was with me in the car and he asked me about the Supreme Court and who was one of the first justices. I couldn't believe that he actually asked me about what the Supreme Court does, since I have never actually discussed it with him in detail (he's only six!).

His next question was, *"Who was the very 1st President?"* When I told him it was George Washington, he put his hands over his mouth in excitement and said, *"I love him!"* This led to a conversation about the three branches of government and what the role of each branch was. I described each branch as simple as possible and amazingly, he actually understood what I was talking about.

Even though we've talked in great detail with our kids about the life of George Washington and the fact that he was the first President, we also keep in mind that we have to keep our Christian Heritage at the forefront of our conversations with our kids or they will forget it.

To be honest, you can't just explain America's Christian Heritage one time to your kids and then expect them to remember. We have found that we have to review a lot of the information over and over with them (mainly the younger ones) regularly in order for it to stick!

THE BOTTOM LINE

We are certainly not the kind of homeschoolers who look down on other families who choose a different education model...quite the opposite in fact. We believe that homeschooling is not for everyone. Each family must find the path that is best for them and use the methods that most effectively allows them to fulfill God's purpose and mission for their specific family.

Homeschooling has worked out great for us and fits our lifestyle and family mission right now. It gives us the flexibility to travel with Rick when he speaks or pack up the bus and leave for a few days without getting a truancy letter from our school district!

One of the best homeschooling suggestions we have ever heard was to put a large laminated map of the United States on the dinner table! This has spurred more conversations about where a particular country, ocean, or lake is located. This photo was taken when the kids were looking up one of the international teams they had just watched play in the Little League World Series. Sometimes the kids will find a really strange name on the map and, of course, it starts the giggle boxes!

3

Rick

In our society today, very few families are blessed with a profession where the children can literally work alongside the parents.

One of the advantages of past agrarian cultures is that your son or daughter could be right by your side in the field even at a young age.

Today, unfortunately, most kids have no idea what their parents really do for a career. They might know the title, such as lawyer or baker or teacher, but they could not give you any description of the details or what their parents actually encounter during any given day.

Whatever your chosen career is, find a way to include your children. You do not have to wait until they are fifteen or eighteen. An eight or nine, or even a six year old, will soak up more than you can imagine!

I love to see families working together for a common purpose. Seeing unity in a family, whether it's running a business together, traveling as missionaries, or worshiping together - I believe that's got to be one of God's greatest joys.....seeing a purpose driven family.

In our case, it was pretty easy and natural to have the kids there with me. I had often heard my mentor, David Barton, and his children talk about the years on the road when the kids were

Rick & David Barton on set of WallBuilders Live!

young, and I always wanted my children to have the same experiences.

YOUNG ROAD WARRIORS

When Trey was about 5, he started traveling with me to speaking engagements. He has always been mature for his age and he proved quickly he could handle himself very well in front of people. From the time all of our kids were small (around 4 yrs. old) we have

Reagan, Rick, & Trey

taught them to introduce themselves to people by looking up into their eyes and shaking their hand firmly. They will need to know how to do this throughout life and it just makes sense for kids to begin this basic life skill when they're young.

Trey learned early on how to interact with people because we took him with us to all of our campaign events even when he was only a year and half old. Everyone wanted to talk to him and hug on him wherever we went.

The Republican Party primary election of March, 1998, became sort of a coming out party for

Trey at the ripe ol' age of twenty-one months. I had no opponent in the primary, so we hosted all the other republican candidates for a victory party that evening. Even with several hundred people in attendance, Trey kept asking to go up to the front microphone when I would announce election results that were coming in from across the state.

Finally, I stacked several chairs behind the podium and stood him up in the top chair and asked if he had anything to say to the people. Oh boy, none of us expected what came next!

It was as if he had memorized the mannerisms of every preacher, speaker, and politician he had ever seen. None of us had any earthly idea what he was saying in his one year old gibberish, but it was clear to everyone that he darn sure meant it! One minute he had a serious look and was pointing at people in the crowd as he spoke, then he would lighten up and open his hands and start laughing as if he had just told the most hilarious joke.

After that night, I knew it was only a matter of time before he would steal the show from me.

During my speeches, I have always recited the 56 words found in the heart of the Declaration of Independence. One day, we decided to let Trey memorize those lines so he could say them on stage with me during my next speech. It took him a while to memorize the whole thing and he was really nervous about speaking in front of a crowd.

Trey is our perfectionist and planner (he gets that from Kara) and he would never dream of doing anything without properly preparing for it first. He is a self starter and works very hard to reach a goal.

Even for a guy, he rarely makes a rash decision. Instead, he gets our advice, does his research, and thinks long and hard before making a decision.

He worked on his own to perfect the words out of the Declaration and when he felt ready, he began his own public speaking career at the young age of only 6 years old. From then on, Trey was a hit with every crowd where he spoke. At nine years old, he memorized all 56 Signers of the Declaration of Independence and could even tell you which states they were from. When he was just eleven, he joined me on stage in front of about 10,000 people at an arena of freedom loving Americans and he recited the Declaration.

Trey speaking at a Reagan-Lincoln Day Dinner

The pictures of Trey and Reagan were taken at a Reagan-Lincoln Day Dinner in 2009 where the kids were asked to speak (note – Dad was not asked to speak, the kids were! I told you they were going to steal the show!)

A few years after Trey had been hitting the circuit with me, Reagan asked if he could also say a part, so he and Trey started sharing the stage.

Reagan is our kid who has very natural talent in everything that he does and most everything he tries comes easily to him. He does not have a worry in the world and you could tell him at the last minute that he is going to speak in front of thousands of people and he would say, *"Great! Show me the stage!"*

He goes with the flow and is our "people person" of the group. Even at a young age, he took to the stage with complete ease and confidence. I remember one time we were talking about what he wanted to be when he grows up and with all seriousness, he said,

"Well, I plan on being a professional baseball player, but if I don't do that, I'll settle for being President." I had to chuckle to myself and give him credit for having such high goals already. He certainly does not lack confidence.

Then along comes Kamryn, our daughter. From the time Kamryn was little bitty, she loved to sing and you could hear her sing all the way across to the other end of the house (or to a neighbor's house ☺). Her voice carries faaaarrr!! We spent the first five years of her life always telling her to lower her voice.

The Commander in Chief

Along with her big voice comes a big personality. She is a combination of Kara and me in many ways. She likes to be organized and know every detail of everything (that's Kara!). She also has a type A personality where she likes to be in charge and tell her brothers what they need to do. She's as smart as they come and probably has more determination in her than all three of our boys combined. Once she sets her mind on a goal, nothing stops her from getting there.

Kara and I always joke that she will be able to work for me and run my office by the time she's thirteen. I'm sure she would love getting paid to tell me what to do every day!

When it was time to add a part for Kamryn on stage, we knew immediately that she should sing and *America the Beautiful* was the perfect fit. God has blessed Kamryn with a voice for singing and I can't wait to see what all God has in store for her. This picture is at our book table at one of our engagements. Kamryn is one of our very hardest workers and she jumps in there and can run the credit card machine and autograph books at the same time!

In charge!

The last of our crew is Rhett or Rhettaroosky as we call him. He is a wonderful combination of all of us. He pays attention to detail like Trey, he has all the confidence in the world like Reagan, and he has determination like Kamryn. Add all of that with a big smile, and he can melt your heart! He might end up being the future politician in the

Rhett ready to fight for Texas!

family. He also loves to sign books! He will sit for hours signing books with me, and trust me, he gets as many requests as I do when it comes to autographs!

Rhett signed books for hours while I looked on

Last year when we were on a trip, Rhett started reciting the Declaration out of the blue. We all looked at each other asking who had taught him that. He smiled and shrugged his shoulders like it was no big deal and he said he had learned it on his own. He had heard his brothers say it so many times that the words just flowed from him. We were thrilled at his self learning style and he immediately started sharing the stage with the rest of the family.

Now, when I'm asked to speak, our kids are requested too! It has truly become a family affair!

We also take our kids to political rallies or Republican conventions and dinners, and you will always see us at the polls on Election Day holding signs for candidates that we support.

We want our children to learn at a young age  that it is their duty to be involved in the process, even if it just means voting. In this picture, we were at an Austin Tea Party where I was asked to speak. The kids all got to stand on stage and hold signs. Even though it was very hot that day, thousands of people showed up and let their voice be heard. They have also been one of the main attractions at other tea parties, where their recitation of the Declaration reminds us all about our founding principles.

When Trey was born in June of '96, Kara and I asked our midwife if we could take Trey to the Republican State Convention, which was only seven days away. She gave us a stern look of disapproval, but I really wanted to hear Alan Keyes speak and could not think of a better way to introduce Trey to the world of politics (at one week old).

Trey

So, against our midwife's orders, we went to the convention and I was beaming as I showed off our newest addition to everyone. After the convention, we were given a certificate stating that Trey was officially the youngest honorary delegate to the convention that year.

The kids were waiting backstage while
the National Anthem was being sung.

Now that Trey is a young man, it is such a blessing to see him really understand the issues that we stand for as a family and as a country. Not only does he understand them, but he has his own opinions and reasons why he believes them too. It is such a joy to see him coming to his own conclusions as he learns what the proper role of government should be in our lives.

Kamryn and her uncle, Kevin Myers, singing his song
"Freedom's Frame" at the Patriot Academy graduation while
Trey and Rhett watch the accompanying slide show

PART II
FROM THE CAMPAIGN TO THE CAPITOL

…..My grace is sufficient for thee: for my strength is
made perfect in weakness.

2 Corinthians 12:9

TO RUN OR NOT TO RUN

★

4

Kara

Rick's passion for influencing the culture through the political process started at a young age. When he was attending Angelo State University in West Texas, he started a college Republican club on campus that grew into the largest, most active Republican club the college had ever seen. During college, he also organized and promoted a "support the troops" rally on campus that drew hundreds of people from all over the city, including local TV stations.

Rick set a personal goal to graduate with his undergraduate degree in two years and he met that goal. He was then accepted to the University of Texas Law School at the age of 20, becoming the youngest law student on campus that year.

He was also continually involved in helping candidates in some way. When Rick makes up his mind to do something, he does it with everything he's got. My point in all of that information is to say that when we got married, I knew how much he had accomplished at a young age and how deeply he loved our nation and wanted to influence our generation to preserve freedom. I knew deep down that politics was somewhere in our future. I didn't know exactly when or how, but it was always in the back of my mind.

With Jack Kemp, author of the Kemp/Roth tax cuts of 1981

So, I was not surprised at all when in 1997 he came home from a political event and said the political director of the Republican Party of Texas had encouraged him to run for the Texas House of Representatives.

Over the course of several months, we sought advice, prayer, and guidance from our families, our pastor, our friends, and key political activists. I think some of our family members thought we were crazy for doing it, but mostly we got their support.

Together we came to the decision that the timing was right for us to run and it fit into our overall goal of making a difference in our state. I knew that when Rick made the final decision to run for office, he would commit 1,000% and that meant jumping on board the train because it was taking off at warp speed....and boy did it ever!

Looking back, we didn't have a clue what we were actually getting ourselves into, but by the grace of God, we persevered through 1 ½ years of tough campaigning throughout our district. In the end, the entire "Green Team" was able to reap the rewards of the hard work of many volunteers who tirelessly walked door to door campaigning for us, stuffing thousands of mailers, and walked in dozens of parades holding "Vote For Rick Green" signs.

One thing that always made Rick different from other candidates is that he never said "I" or "me." It was always "we" and "us." In other words, it was not about him…it was about the team, about the

Rick with supporters and prayer partners Kirvin & Beckie Griffin

people and their representation. That was not some conjured up political strategy…it was Rick straight from the heart.

Where I would prefer to have dinner alone with Rick and the kids, he prefers to invite everyone within shouting distance. He hates to see anyone left out and is constantly looking for ways to include people in the cause.

Over 1,000 people would show up to
our big fundraiser every year

This sincere motivation to give people an outlet for their patriotism might explain why our annual campaign dinner was the largest in Texas, even bigger and more exciting than statewide candidates. People were drawn to Rick because of his plain spoken, uncompromising conviction. But they stayed a part of the team because it was exactly that…a team!

We were often brought to tears by the level of sacrifice and generosity we saw in people because they believed in the same values as us and they were excited to be a part of something that would make a positive difference for our state.

Family, friends, and supporters who showed up to
many parades throughout the district

5

Kara

Once we made the decision in 1997 to run, our lives changed overnight. Meetings were being set up every day with statewide Republicans, businessmen, political consultants, and every person in the district we could get to take a meeting.

We filed the paperwork to set up a treasurer and appointed my mom to fill that position. We were then able to start raising money for the campaign. So much started happening so fast. For the most part in the beginning, it was just Rick and me running everything. I was taking care of the details and he was raising money and asking for votes.

We knew immediately that God was opening doors for us that we could never open ourselves. Meetings with many prominent people were being set up that we could have never made happen on our own and every day new people were coming into our lives who would become life-long friends and supporters. There is  really no way to fully prepare yourself for the whirlwind of campaigning when it's your first time out there, but we had a strong support system of family and friends that made the process easier.

We were definitely the underdogs in the race. We were running against a powerful Democrat incumbent who was a nice guy, but not representing the conservative values that reflected our district. We wholeheartedly believed that the timing was right for our district to change hands and that Rick would best represent the families and businesses in our community by talking about the three most important things to us: Faith, Family, & Freedom. That was our campaign motto and every statewide issue came back to one of those three things.

1998 Campaign Mailer

A POTENT COMBINATION

We had our official campaign kick off in early 1997 (1 ½ years before the general election) outside at a local restaurant in our hometown. We had a decent

showing of people for our first event and it was at that little restaurant in Dripping Springs where we discovered the very magical combination of the Kyle Family music and Rick's very passionate, articulate speeches.

**The Kyle Family is joined by Johnny Gimble &
Sammy Alred at one of our fundraisers**

Rick called my family's singing his "secret
weapon" because their mix of gospel and country set
the stage perfect for the traditional values message of
Rick's campaign. The word started getting out across
the district that there was a young, conservative
Republican named Rick Green that was going to be a
serious contender in the race for State Representative.

Rick is the kind of person who wears his heart
and his beliefs on his sleeve. He's never met a stranger
and he instantly became liked on the campaign trail.
He really enjoys getting to meet new people wherever
we go, and I think that the genuine nature of his

personality and his enthusiasm drew people to him instantly. It has always amazed me how easily he can walk up to a stranger, shake their hand, and strike up a conversation.

By the summer of 1997, all we were doing was campaigning full time. Rick was trying to keep us afloat financially by doing legal work when he wasn't campaigning. Our days and weeks

Always working the room!

were jammed packed with meetings, designing with printers, candidate forums, walking neighborhoods, walking in parades, recruiting volunteers, and the list goes on! We kept this pace up for the rest of the year.

THE GOON SQUAD STRIKES

I can vividly remember during that time, we went out of town for a few days to visit Rick's family.

We had converted our garage into our campaign office and we had two computers that Rick and I and some of the campaign volunteers used for all of our campaign work. We had voter lists on them, as well as our long term campaign plan that went into detail about our financial goals for the year. These computers contained our personal contact lists and many other campaign documents.

When we got home, it was late into the night. Trey was only a year old and was fast asleep in the car as we pulled into the driveway.

We walked in the front door and eventually made our way into the office. That's when we noticed that our house had been broken into and both campaign computers had been stolen. Nothing else had been touched.

It was obvious that the computers were the only thing they were interested in taking. We called our sheriff's department and they came out to our house and took our statements and dusted for fingerprints.

Unfortunately, nothing ever turned up and we still don't know who was involved in breaking into our house.

That was a real wake up call for us. At that moment, we realized just how vulnerable we were and how we could not let our guard down for anything.

If someone was willing to break in and steal our computers over politics, what else were they capable of doing?

GRASSROOTS MADE THE DIFFERENCE

We were very blessed throughout the campaign to meet some of the dearest people who worked tirelessly for us. They made phone calls, stuffed thousands of mailers, walked in dozens of parades, stood at the polls on Election Day holding signs, and most importantly kept us in their prayers. We relied so much on their friendship and support and still do to this day.

It was not uncommon for 50 to 100 people to volunteer their day for us in a parade, walking in the heat, giving out campaign material, and winning votes. When the Green Team came over the hill in a parade, it looked like an invasion! This particular photo is from our 2002 campaign.

Rick's mom, Pat, even moved in for a few months to help us with the mailers and she is pictured here getting some help from our unofficial campaign manager, Trey!

It truly was a family affair. My grandfather spent day after day out in our shed building our yard signs. We lost count at nearly 1,000 signs being built by him alone during the campaign. The picture above is my grandparents, Skeeter & Barbara, campaigning with Trey using the signs built by Skeeter.

By May of 1998, we were only six months away from the election, and the base of our supporters and the excitement surrounding the campaign was growing daily. By now, Rick was becoming known not just in our district, but all across the State of Texas.

STRESS? WHAT STRESS?

Our life is always chaotic and it seems like even when we have more to do than we can ever accomplish, we somehow find a way to make it even more chaotic! This was definitely the case when we sold our house right in the heat of the campaign.

We had always wanted to build on the land that my grandparents had bought in Dripping Springs. So when we got a contract on our house, we didn't want to pass up the chance to move and build the house that our kids would grow up in. The bad part was that after we signed the contract, we had only 30 days to move and we didn't have a house to move into!

Most normal people would have rented a house or an apartment to live in while their house was being built. And certainly any normal person would finish the campaign before starting to build a house. But not us! We had to do it the most stressful way imaginable.

Being the conservative that he is, Rick decided that he didn't want to throw money away on rent for six months, so he made up his mind that we would build a small "guest house" that we could live in "for a while" and then add on to it one day.

I don't recall which state official Trey was calling in
the photo above, but I'm sure it was important!

All I can say is thank the good Lord that we were so young. I was only 23 at the time and Rick was 27. We worked around the clock clearing land and setting the form for the foundation to be laid. If there was ever a time where we "physically" almost killed ourselves, it was during those 30 days. We hired out what we couldn't do ourselves (like the septic and water well) and at the end of 30 days, believe it or not, we had a small "guest house" to move into.

THE HOME STRETCH

Now it was time to get focused back on the campaign. Our pace picked up once again and it seemed like we had volunteers coming and going from our house all the time. We again converted our garage into a campaign office and that is where we stuffed mailers, made get out the vote calls, and coordinated all the logistics for the campaign.

About this time we started making decisions about what kind of campaign commercial we would run on TV during the last few weeks of the election.

Trey was now two and had become a campaign favorite.

Everywhere we went he would give a thumbs up and say *"Vote My Daddy!"* People loved him! So we decided that he just had to be on the commercial saying *"Vote My Daddy!"* and giving his famous thumbs

up. President Bush (who was Governor at the time) told us after the election that he remembered our commercial more than anyone else's because of Trey. We're still convinced that it was his cute smile that won the election for us.

AMAZING ENDORSEMENTS

Rick was also very blessed to be able to secure endorsements from Senator Phil Gramm and Zig Ziglar. Later, in our second campaign, he would also receive personal

Zig & Rick with his lifelong friend Kit Courrege & his wife, Lori

endorsement commercials from Charlton Heston and Alan Keyes. Looking back, it is so clear how God just opened every door necessary for us to have a successful campaign. Although Rick was an

exceptional candidate, we were still young and had not proven ourselves in politics yet. None of our volunteers or our endorsers had to go out on a limb and give their endorsement, but they did and we will always be grateful for that.

Our district included three counties and it took about 2 hours to get from one end of the district to the other. There were many days when we would go to different events in all three counties, and at the end of the day we would crawl into bed exhausted.

A HEART BREAKING MOMENT

During this hectic schedule, I found out I was pregnant. I had gotten so busy that I had lost track of time and it didn't dawn on me that I was exhausted because I was pregnant. We were elated and couldn't wait to give Trey a brother or sister for him to grow up with. This was in September – two months before the election.

In the Christian life, there is a special recognition of the gift of life and an acknowledgment that it comes from God. There must also be a recognition that God is sovereign even when events do not go the way we wish, or when tragedy strikes.

In the final weeks of the campaign, I started bleeding and feared the worst. I called my midwife to let her know, although I already knew what she would say. She said it sounded like I was miscarrying and one week later I did. That was a hard blow and it definitely took the wind out of our sails. We had been so excited about the progress of the campaign and the news of a new baby, and then the miscarriage just put everything into perspective about what was important in life.

We finished the last two months of the campaign with everything we had and prayed in the end that we had done everything we physically could to win. There are so many people who we should recognize for their part in contributing to the campaign, but my biggest thanks goes to my mom, Nelda Kyle. She was the rock (and still continues

Kara's Grandmother, Kamryn, & Kara's mom

to be) that Rick and I were able to depend on for babysitting, meals, last minute errands, late night stuffing parties, and a host of other things. She's always ready to do what's asked of her and never asks for anything in return. We wouldn't have been able to make it through the whole campaign process and stay sane without the support of our family.

Now it was Election Day and we would see if all the hard work had paid off.

ELECTION DAY

We woke up before daylight and had a team of volunteers ready to drive to every polling location in the district to stake our big campaign signs in the ground. It was hard to believe that after all the hard work the big day was finally here.

Rick, Trey, and I spent most of the day in Gonzales County which was the county farthest away. We had stayed the night before with several of our volunteers in the home of our strongest Gonzales supporter, Myrna McLeroy, so we could be up at 4:00 AM to get signs out at all the polling locations.

We then stood at the polls there and shook hands with voters until the very last person had entered the building. Once the polls had closed, we went to the Gonzales Republican headquarters to thank our supporters and then we made our way back towards Hays County where we had planned on spending the evening watching the election results come in with friends and family.

When we started campaigning the year before, I can honestly say that we thought we would either win big or lose big, but we never dreamed we would end up on the roller coaster ride that lay ahead of us.

Following the unusual drama of election night (detailed in the next chapter), we would soon learn the best news of all...I was pregnant again and about 8 months later we had our second son, Reagan Kyle Green.

Reagan was a natural campaigner from the start and has become known as Rick's "mini-me"

OUR AMERICAN STORY

6

Rick

(Excerpt from Rick's book *Freedom's Frame*)

HANGING CHADS BEFORE THEY WERE COOL

It was around midnight on election night in 1998, when my campaign manager brought me the news that we had been waiting for since the polls closed. The final numbers were in from the election clerks of the three counties in our district and they showed that thirty thousand people had voted in our race and we had lost by twenty votes.

Twenty votes!

The guy standing next to me said, *"Twenty votes? I could have gotten you twenty more votes Rick!"* That was probably not the best timing or the wisest thing for him to say to me, but I restrained myself from laying hands on him that night (and not for prayer). But he was right. After all, twenty votes is just one *decent* size Texas home school family! Kara and I home school our four children (or I should say Kara home schools our four children) and friends who have many more children than us, like to encourage us by saying, *"Nice start you got going there!"*

As the news spread of the extremely narrow margin of votes by which I had lost the election, I began to receive hundreds of phone calls from supporters who were all asking me to request a recount. In Texas, we have a statute that authorizes a recount when a race is this close. So, at their prompting I decided to ask that the votes would be counted again.

The recount was to be done one county at a time, and we started with the most democrat county in the district. My team knew nothing about the recount process. Recall the year. This was 1998, two years before the world would learn all about recounts and hanging chads in the Florida presidential election. I was the only attorney on the team; the rest were either family members or volunteers from my church and other churches in the district. So, you can imagine our level of intimidation when we arrived at the start of the recount and faced the incumbent's team of high-powered attorneys. But what we lacked in one area we made up for in another—we had a team who was praying around the clock, and a group of dedicated volunteers who were ready to stay as long as it took to make sure that every ballot was counted correctly.

VOTE BY VOTE

By the end of the recount of that first county, we had picked up three votes. The next morning, we counted the second county and picked up another four votes. As I was driving over to the third county where Kara and our family team were getting ready for the last count to begin, I started doing the math in my head.

The first two counties combined were half the size of the third county. So statistically in my mind, we should pick up twice as many votes in the third county as we did in the first two. That could mean fourteen votes added to the seven we already had for a total of twenty-one new votes in all. If so, that would mean that I could win the election by a ONE vote victory!

My mind was reeling on the way to the courthouse where the final count was to take place—I must have broken every traffic law in the book that day. When I arrived, I saw the six tables that had been set up for the recount teams. Each side was allowed to have one representative per table.

For the first half hour or so, not much happened. Then Chad Hudson, Kara's cousin, whispered to me that we had just picked up four votes at his table. A friend of the family, Brian Wittmuss, came and told me we had just picked up another five votes. Now that we were down to a margin of eleven votes, the attorneys on the other side were starting to sweat. They had probably assured their client—the incumbent—that a recount would not change the election because it had not happened in more than twenty years!

The whirlwind continued for the next couple of hours. Kara's aunt brought news of twelve more votes, my mother-in-law announced another ten, then someone else from another table said we had just lost seven, and on it went until it was finally over, and we had picked up forty-nine additional votes in that one county. Combined with the votes

Green gains 56 votes in recount, enough to win!

By Bob Ochoa
View Staff

Dripping Springs Republican Rick Green emerged the unofficial winner Thursday night in a recount of the tight race for state representative between Green and two-term incumbent Democrat Alec Rhodes.

The recount, which Green requested last week after losing to Rhodes by only 20 votes in the November 3 election, began Monday in Gonzales County and was completed in Hays and Caldwell Counties late Thursday afternoon.

A jubilant Green told the View Thursday evening he had gained more than 50 votes in the recount, throwing the election unofficially in his favor by about a 35-vote margin.

"I'm very surprised we won," Green said. "After the election (November 3) I didn't think it would turn but I'm happily surprised. It is God's will, not mine."

Rick Green

we picked up in the recount of the other two counties,

we had a combined total of fifty-six additional votes. This meant that I went from losing the election by twenty votes, to winning it by thirty-six.

Two months later with Trey in my arms, I took the oath of office in the Texas

House of Representatives. President Bush (Governor of Texas at the time) nicknamed me *"Landslide Green,"* which he thought was very funny in 1998. However, it was probably not making him smile all that much when in the 2000 election we all had to wait for the Florida returns to be recounted to know who would be the next President of the United States. That year, the presidential election was decided by a narrow margin of 537 votes.

EVERY VOTE COUNTS!

So, never buy the lie that your one vote does not count. Voting is the best way for you to have your voice heard and your values counted. Remember, our nation does not elect the leaders that a majority of its citizens prefer. It elects the leaders that a majority of the citizens *who show up to vote* choose! If you don't vote, you don't count.

★

7

Rick

On January 12th, 1999, I was sworn in as a State Representative on the floor of the Texas House of Representatives as the youngest freshman for that year. I will never forget the awe of that day and the weight and responsibility of what I was about to embark upon.

Kara, our parents, and our pastor, were squeezed into chairs close to my desk on the House Floor. As I sat down after the oath, it began to dawn on me that I was now one of only 181 people making laws for the State of Texas.

About that time, my dad leaned over and said, *"This sure is a long way from the backwoods of Salem, Arkansas."* I knew he was proud of me, but I had not thought about what we were experiencing in the context of family history.

My best friend, Dad.

I was the first of both my mom and my dad's families to graduate from college. My dad wanted me to go to law school since I was fifteen, always wanting me to have advantages he did not have.

My Grandparents holding my dad & Aunt Linda

The poor in our nation today live like kings of yesterday compared to how my dad grew up. His family was very loving and no one complained about what they did not have and they certainly did not ask others, including the government, to provide for them. I'm extremely proud of where I come from and the values my grandparents passed down to us. They were not rich in finances, but they were wealthy in spirit, love, and American work ethic.

Considering the dirt floors and lack of indoor plumbing my dad grew up with, that day sitting in the Texas Capitol was something like Dorothy finding her way to Oz.

It would not be long before I pulled back the curtain and found the "wizards" of state government were just ordinary men and women like you and me.

The truth is that I was both pleasantly surprised and sorely disappointed with the caliber of people I came to know in the halls of the Capitol.

On one hand, I was thrilled to find many Godly men and women serving their state out of a sense of devotion and duty and doing so with a Biblical worldview.

My desk mate, Charlie Howard, became a good friend & mentor

On the other hand, I too often found myself asking about other men and women, *"How in the world did they ever win an election and how has our state survived with them making decisions for us?"*

I've been cussed out, choked, ridiculed, shouted down, booed, and hissed by fellow Members of the Legislature, not to mention members of the lobby. But I've also been prayed for, shared tears of joy and pain, supported, encouraged, and applauded by other Members. This would be a good time for Forrest

Gump to say something about life being like a box of chocolates, but let me just say that it takes all kinds. The makeup of legislators is no different than your family, local club, high school class, or church group.

One of my colleagues was so right when he told me, *"For the first two weeks you are here at the Capitol,*

you will wonder how in the world you got here. After being around the rest of us for two weeks, you'll be asking how in the world WE got here!"

HITTING THE GROUND RUNNING

As we began to put the team together, I received two very different pieces of advice on hiring staff. One school of thought was to hire experienced

Capitol staffers who knew the ropes since I was new. The other path was to hire people I knew well and trusted, people that did not already have an agenda and allegiances I was unaware of.

I chose the second school of thought. My first hire was a longtime friend and business associate, Greg Tolen, whom I trusted with my life and who I knew shared my conservative principles. I remember him saying, *"But Rick, I don't have any idea how to run a legislative office."* I said, *"Hey, we'll learn together!"*

Greg & Darlene Tolen have become the best of friends & fellow patriots

Next, we hired two ladies who had been very valuable to us on the campaign trail.

The picture from our campaign scrapbook on the next page says it all. Rita Steitle had shown up out of nowhere and literally volunteered full time for the critical last month or so of the campaign. She was a retired legal secretary with fiery conservative convictions that made even me look weak sometimes! I vividly remember on Election Day standing next to her pickup, pictured to the right, begging and pleading to convince her that the world could not be saved without her on my team at the

Capitol if we won! She said only for 6 months just to get me through my first Session and get my feet on the ground. When that was over, I begged some more and actually kept her from going back into retirement for a couple of years. She has always been such a blessing to the Green family!

Deidra Voigt had become one of my strongest supporters in Gonzales County, but it was not overnight. Most all of my supporters joined the Green Team after hearing me give a speech, but not with Deidra! Oh no, she still reminds me these days that it took THREE times of hearing me speak before she was convinced I was the "real deal!" But once she was committed to the team, she was our most outspoken advocate!

Left to right: Deidra Voigt, Rita Steitle, then Gov. George Bush, Rick, & Greg Tolen

My sister-in-law, Kimberly, came aboard as scheduler and our team was ready to go.

I felt like I had surrounded myself by staff whom I could fully trust and who would always put ethics above any political agenda. Putting the wrong people around you can literally ruin you, but in our case our team was so thorough and effective that we got calls from people in other districts asking us to help them because their own State Rep. wasn't responding to their calls.

We set our goals high for what we wanted to accomplish and our team wasted no time jumping in there and working on the conservative agenda upon which we had campaigned.

Press Conference with Reps. Myra Crownover, Charlie Howard, & Wayne Christian

In my first Session, the Texas Legislature passed parental notification of abortion, tort reform, and other conservative measures. But the piece of the agenda where I got to run point was protecting our Second Amendment rights.

GOD & GUNS

In 1999, several liberal state attorney generals, many large cities, and the Clinton Administration were suing gun manufacturers under the ridiculous theory that they were to blame for crime.

Let's think about that for a moment. You legally buy a gun at Wal-Mart. The gun was legally manufactured and sold. Some nut breaks into your home, steals the gun, then goes out and commits a crime with it. Now we give the following multiple choice question to a liberal politician and ask who is to blame for the crime:

   A.   The criminal who chose to break the law and use the weapon in an illegal way.

   B.   You, the law abiding legal purchaser of the weapon.

   C.   The criminal's 2nd grade teacher who fifteen years ago responded to the criminals eight year old temper tantrum by putting the criminal in detention rather than taking the criminal through years of therapy at taxpayer expense.

D. Smith & Wesson, for making a legal product that is used five times as often in the U.S. to stop a crime as it is used to commit a crime.

Of course, the liberal politician's eyes glaze over answer A. They immediately love to blame everyone in answers B, C, and D. Unable to make the blame stick on you or the teacher, they went after the deep pockets of the gun manufacturer.

In the first few days of the Legislative Session, I read where another state was passing legislation to prevent cities in their state from joining the liberal blame game and sue gun makers. Because cities get their authority from the state and because these actions were bankrupting U.S. gun manufacturers just trying to defend the ridiculous, yet expensive, lawsuits, we jumped on the idea.

We filed our legislation and the firestorm (pun intended) began immediately. Houston and Dallas were already planning to enter the fray of lawsuits, so their legislative delegations were quickly against us.

Of course the liberal media hated the bill and began calling me a *"God and Guns"* conservative (which happens to be a label I appreciate) because I used such outlandish phrases as *"the God given right to keep and bear arms."*

This was just my way of explaining what the Founding Fathers had said regarding the Biblical right of self-protection as being something given by our Creator, not by our government. Needless to say, I was quickly hated by the media and the rest of the left wing, but strongly supported by conservatives.

LET THE GAMES BEGIN

After much wrangling behind the scenes, our bill finally got out of committee and made its way to the House Calendar. It was first up to be debated, so I stayed up almost all of the night before preparing for what would be my first debate on the House Floor.

When the Speaker called me forward to present the bill, I was both nervous and excited. I had thoroughly prepared, so I was also confident I was ready for the arguments that would be thrown at me.

The Texas House has two podiums and microphones. The author of a bill goes to the front microphone and anyone wanting to question the author goes to the back microphone. When a controversial bill is called up, the opposition quickly lines up at the back microphone ready to throw their best at the author.

As I approached the front mic ready to give my best ten minute speech on why this bill was important, I noticed that none of the opposition was at the back microphone.

A more senior Member had told me on another day, *"If the opposition to one of your bills doesn't show up and you know you have the votes on the floor, put aside your ego and great speech and simply ask for passage."*

So that is exactly what I did. As bad as I wanted to give that speech I had worked so hard to prepare, the advice of that senior Member rang in my ears.

I simply gave a ten second description of the bill, which everyone in Austin was already familiar with, and then said, *"Mr. Speaker, I move passage."*

Speaker of the House Pete Laney, though a Democrat, was pretty good on gun issues and supported

Speaker Laney & Rick

the bill. So he simply said, *"Mr. Green moves passage, are there any objections? Hearing none, SB717 is passed."*

Several supporters of the bill came up congratulating me and saying great job, but it sure felt anti-climatic to me after staying up all night to prepare.

However, the battle was not yet over. Each bill has to pass twice on the House Floor, so our bill would come up again the next day for passage once again. The good news for me at this point was that any amendment the next day would require 2/3's rather than a simple majority like the first day a bill is debated.

Rep. Ron Wilson (D) became a good friend & partner on issues like guns and school choice

But I'm getting ahead of the story.

About fifteen minutes later, the leaders of the opposition started filing onto the House Floor and heading to the back microphone asking the Speaker if our bill had been brought up yet. When informed by the Speaker that the bill had, in fact, been brought up and had, in fact, already passed, the opposition was less than happy.

Apparently, the opposition leaders were simply late to the House Chamber that morning and missed their opportunity to fully question me about the bill. There was much debate, some heated, over whether or not the bill should be brought back up for consideration since they were late. The Speaker ruled that they missed their chance, but could dive in on our second day of debating the bill.

The next day would not be so easy.

When I was called by the Speaker to lay out my bill for the second time and final passage, this time the opposition was already lined up at the back microphone armed and ready (with arguments, not Colt or Smith & Wesson!).

I was only about two sentences into my opening statement when the opposition first interrupted with, "Mr. *Speaker, will the gentleman yield for a question."*

Standing at the back microphone was probably the best debater in the Texas House. Think Alan Keyes and Ronald Reagan rolled into one and you get the idea. This guy could rhyme like a rapper and when he started to sing, you were just dead in the water.

His first line of questioning was about the tobacco lawsuits a few years before where states had sued all the cigarette manufacturers and won billions. He wanted to know if I had supported that effort.

Well, just for the record, I absolutely did not support the lawsuits because it was just another strike against personal responsibility and an attempt to shift the blame away from individuals for their own decisions.

But I knew he was leading me into a trap, so I tried to diffuse it with a little humor. All the Members often ribbed me about being so young, so I had taken to making fun of myself in that regard to show it didn't bother me.

I said something to him about me not being involved in that tobacco debate because I was probably still in High School at the time.  As he started to respond, I could feel the rhythm building in his words and I knew I was in for it now.

He started with something like, *"Well, Mr. Green, you're a big boy now. And you're here in the big boy House with your big boy colleagues dealing with big boy issues. So now it's time for you to be a big boy and debate with the big boys."*

It was one of those moments where the whole chamber had grown silent and I felt like it was time to sink or swim. The gallery was full of lobbyists and staff, watching and wondering the same thing as the chamber full of Members. They were wondering if the kid from Dripping Springs was going to melt or not.

I said the only thing that popped into my head, *"Yes, Mr. Turner, and big boys show up on time to debate."*

A big smile spread across his face and after a pause, he very graciously responded, *"Touché, touché Mr. Green."* The chamber and gallery burst into laughter, and we then had a mostly friendly debate for three full hours. We defeated every negative amendment that came at us and it was an exhilarating experience to be a part of the team that won the day.

My opponent that day became a friend and by the end of the debate, I earned the respect of my colleagues as at least a halfway decent debater on the House Floor. The former Speaker of the House said it was the best he'd ever seen, but he was lobbying for the NRA, so I think he was just happy the bill passed!

There would be other days when my star did not shine so bright. Most battles I fought in those days were lost to a liberal democrat majority, but our side always chose to keep fighting.

One of my favorite memories was when Trey was with me on the House Floor one day. He was only three years old but he looked so grown up in his coat and his cowboy boots on. My good friend, Rep. Ron Wilson, came up to Trey, knelt down on a knee in front of him and looked him over from head to toe. He then shook his head slowly and said, *"Boy, we're gonna get rid of your boots and turn you into a city slicker today."*

At lunch time, Rep. Wilson went on a little shopping spree and when the House convened that afternoon, he found Trey at my desk and pulled out a pair of Nike Air Jordan high tops and a Fubu football Jersey. When Trey saw the shoes and jersey, his response was *"cool"* and Ron said, *"That's more like it!"* Right there on the House Floor in the middle of session, Rep. Wilson helped Trey get changed into his new city slicker outfit! Trey gave him a "five" and a hug, and that jersey is still getting passed down from Green boy to Green boy in our family. Trey thought Rep. Wilson was the coolest guy he had ever met after that!

ROUND TWO

The 2000 campaign was a landslide victory for us as we received almost 60% of the vote. We stayed up nearly all night long waiting to see if Governor Bush would defeat Al Gore, but it would be weeks before we got the answer to that question!

Not usually ones for pomp and fluff, we decided to make an exception and travel to Washington, D.C. for President Bush's Inauguration.

In Washington DC at President Bush's Inauguration

After returning from the festivities, I started working on the 2001 Legislative Session with high hopes.

Kara's Grandfather and Trey sat with me for
the 2001 Swearing In Ceremony.

Trey took the oath with me like a pro!

Our team was becoming more and more effective, which in turn, brought heightened attacks from the left. We could feel the heat getting turned up, but we had absolutely no idea just how bad it would get.

A DREAM COME TRUE

I was speaking more and more around the state and David Barton had begun talking with me about filling in for him once in awhile for WallBuilder Presentations about the Founding Fathers.

David's many audio cassettes about the Founders had been my "university on wheels" in my pickup truck for years. I had memorized as much as I could and began talking about the Founding Fathers in my speeches. Like most people, my "formal" education in college and in law school was completely void of the faith of the men and women who founded America.

Well, apparently David's parents, Rose & Grady, heard me speak at a function for conservatives.

I'm pretty sure they must have said, *"David, that kid is stealing all your stuff, you might as well hire him!"*

Seriously, they gave a good report and it opened the door for the most life changing and meaningful professional relationship I've ever had.

David Barton is the real deal. I've learned more from him about history, the Bible, my relationship with Christ, marriage, raising kids, public speaking, and impacting the culture than from everyone else I've known combined.

Presenting David with the *"Champion of the Torch of Freedom"* Award at our 2009 Patriot Academy graduation dinner

As I began to speak for WallBuilders once in awhile, I could feel God leading my heart towards speaking and less and less towards the legislature.

A CAUSE TO PUT MY HEART INTO

But at the moment I was in the middle of a Legislative Session and had a job to do. Early in the Session, I read a poll that said barely half of Texans could name even one of the five freedoms guaranteed in the First Amendment and only 5% could name two.

If we don't even know what our freedoms are, how in the world will we know when they have been violated? How can we stand and defend them?

I proposed and the Legislature eventually passed House Bill 1776. This legislation created *"Celebrate Freedom Week"* in public schools across Texas. During *"Celebrate Freedom Week,"* children study the Founding Fathers and the Declaration of Independence, focusing on the following fifty-six words from the Declaration the Green kids recite on stage every chance they get:

We hold these truths to be self-evident, that all men are created equal, that they are endowed by their Creator with certain unalienable Rights, that among these are Life, Liberty and the pursuit of Happiness. That to secure these rights, Governments are instituted among Men, deriving their just powers from the consent of the governed.

Despite the fact that we cannot teach from the Bible in the classroom, the biblical foundations of our government can be taught. Through these fifty-six words from the heart of the Declaration, we can instill in young people the knowledge that freedom and rights come from God.

Therefore, there must be a Creator, and since freedom comes from Him, government cannot take that freedom away from the individual. The document makes it clear we are created beings and life is an unalienable right that must be protected. "Truths" worth fighting and dying for means moral relativism is wrong. Do you see the possibilities?

A court can interpret our founding documents however it wants, but if students read them and memorize them, they will get the foundation. They will know the truth, and will then be able to recognize the falsehood when courts misinterpret these documents.

Several states have modeled and passed legislation similar to House Bill 1776. You can help get it done in your state or you can make sure your local school district is participating.

When I first passed the law in the spring of 2001, an interesting thing happened. This was six months before 9/11 occurred and people were not nearly as patriotic as they were after 9/11.

In fact, when the education committee passed the bill out, the members on the committee took out little American flags and waived them in a mocking fashion because they thought I was being overly patriotic.

Everyone thought the bill would pass with no problem. I had worked to gather more than one hundred Democrat and Republican co-authors who recognized the need for our children to better learn these basic concepts.

With more than two thirds of the House signing on, passage should have been a cinch, so the education committee sent the bill to the Local and Consent Calendar Committee, rather than the regular Calendars Committee. Both of these committees have the responsibility of setting the calendar for debate on the House Floor. The regular Calendars Committee is perhaps the most powerful committee in the Texas House because your bill never comes up for debate unless  you get it through that committee and any member on that committee can tag your bill to prevent it from being set.

On the other hand, the Local and Consent Calendar is where a bill goes that only affects the author's district or is so non-controversial it will pass with ease, which is what the Education Committee expected with mine. But for some reason, my bill was not getting set on the Local and Consent Calendar to pass the House and go to the Senate.

I finally found out that a member of the committee had a problem with the bill and was holding it up, so I went to visit with him. It turns out he did not like the provision that had children recite the fifty-six words from the heart of the Declaration, even though I had an *"opt out clause"* where a student's parents could opt them out of this activity during Celebrate Freedom Week if they had some reason of conscience to do so.

This state representative, for reasons I still do not understand to this day, exploded with rage telling me, *"You have no right to tell these kids to repeat those things."* The idea of our education system actually taking a position on worldview and instilling the basic strategies of our national success is an abhorrent idea to some. I would have expected this from a left wing democrat, but this guy was a Republican from a conservative district.

Well, the good news is that we finally got the bill passed, although I was forced by this certain state representative to change the wording in the bill from "required" to "permissive". This means that a school district could do it or not do it, and it was up to local

Gov. Perry signs HB1776 into law at a school in my district
and gives the pen to a little girl named "Americus"

citizens to make them do it. In 2003, my friend, Representative Bryan Hughes, modified the statute back to the way I had originally written it so that every school is now required to participate.

Laws like this are difficult to enforce, so if you live in Texas, you can help teach freedom by simply raising the issue with your local school board and find out if they are implementing a Celebrate Freedom Week.

If your state has not passed similar legislation, go visit with your legislators and ask them to join you in the effort to teach freedom.

The language of HB1776 is now making its way into every textbook and classroom in Texas. It has taken nearly 10 years to fully implement the idea, but the positive effects will be felt for generations. I love receiving mail and pictures from kids and teachers from all over the State of Texas and across America as they share with me the activities of their school during Celebrate Freedom Week.

Let the American youth never forget, that they possess a noble inheritance, bought by the toils, and sufferings, and blood of their ancestors; and capacity, if wisely improved, and faithfully guarded, of transmitting to their latest posterity all the substantial blessings of life, the peaceful enjoyment of liberty, property, religion, and independence. —**Joseph Story**

Supreme Court Justice from 1811-1845

TIME WELL SPENT

While there are a couple of votes (out of thousands) I'd probably cast differently today than I did back then, all in all it was a wonderful experience that I would not trade or change.

There are many great memories from my time in the Texas House. One of my absolute favorite days was on March 12, 2001,

which I was privileged to spend with Ian McLain as part of our "page program." The House allows Members to have a young person essentially shadow them for the day and run errands back and forth from the office to the House Floor. Ian hails from a wonderful family in Gonzales, Texas. A healthy boy, he was struck by lightning and miraculously survived.

We passed a House Resolution honoring his courage and I had the privilege of wheeling him as fast as possible around the Capitol in his wheel chair. What an inspiration Ian continues to be!

Another great memory was Easter at the Governor's mansion during our second term. We were late (surprise, surprise) and Trey was very worried that he had missed his chance to participate in the big Easter egg hunt. We walked up after his age group had started, but he managed to still find the coveted golden egg.

Governor Rick Perry & the Greens

We have been able to get to know so many wonderful people we would never have met without those days as a Legislator.

TIME FOR A NEW CHAPTER

When it came to an end on election night 2002, there was a packed room waiting on me to say something. Once again, the race came down to the wire with us losing by a couple hundred votes out of 45,000. Everyone in the room was well aware of the unethical and dishonest way we had been defeated. Deep down, I was actually glad to be moving into a new chapter in my life.

However, as I began to speak, I looked across the sea of faces of individuals and families that had sacrificed so much for our team.

Tracey Dean (left) & his wife Marty, were two of our strongest supporters for years. A successful & very busy businessman, he took time off to stand out in the heat day after day throughout early voting & Election Day. Legendary Texas Longhorn Coach Darrell Royal (right) was another strong supporter.

I'm already a pretty emotional and very passionate guy. I was physically exhausted and emotionally spent. I did my best to choke back the tears, but could not find the words to thank all those people for all they had done. Even now, nearly a decade later, I feel so much gratitude for them and wish I had an adequate way to show my appreciation to them all.

There are SO many people I'd love to tell you about and show you pictures of them from the campaign trail. With limited space, we can only show you these few

Tom Huth, Mary Joe Roddie, & Delbert & Linda Johnston were among our staunchest supporters and often went above and beyond the call of duty!

examples of pictures we were able to find before our publishing deadline!

I am very thankful that the people of Hays, Caldwell, and Gonzales Counties allowed me to serve them in the Texas Legislature.

Trey helps me out on the House Floor

THE GOOD, THE BAD, AND THE UGLY

★

8

Kara

Making the decision to run for any office, whether it's your local school board, city council, or state or federal level, there are several things you should factor in.

First of all, it will cost you your own money. Which level of office you run for will determine how much of your own money you will need to invest. We loaned our first campaign $30,000 and it took us six years to get those loans paid back. However, some candidates never recoup their own expenses.

Second, it takes lots of time to run an effective campaign. The hardest part about running for office, for most people, is that it takes so much time away from your work and your family, especially if you want to do it the right way and win.

The third aspect to consider is your reputation. Anyone who runs for any office needs to be ready to take lots of insults, especially from the media.

When Rick ran for State Rep, we were told by many people to be ready for the outright lies that would be told about us. At first, we didn't believe that people would just make things up about us, but they did. It was definitely an eye opening experience.

WE OWN A LAKE ON A COMPOUND?

At one point after Rick was elected, we heard there was a rumor going around that we owned our own lake and we were pumping precious water from our aquifer that was going dry in order to keep our "lake" full. That one always amused us. When anyone would ask us if that was true, we would laugh and say, *"Wow, we own a whole lake and didn't even know it!"*

Another rumor that went around and still surfaces every once in a while is that we live on a *"compound."* This one is a little closer to reality since we do live on family land that was bought by my grandparents and passed down to their kids with the hopes that their children, grandchildren, and great-grandchildren would one day live near each other.

Trey with his BB gun. Maybe that creek behind him is the mystery lake?

Fortunately, my grandparents got to see that dream become a reality. Our kids have all been able to grow up right down the road from their cousins,

Cousins Lily, Kamryn, Reagan, & Annie

grandparents, great-grandparents, aunts, and uncles.

I guess because we are Christians who live next door to our family and we also happen to be avid hunters, it makes for good conversation to say we live on a *"compound"*.

Rhett & his cousin Luke on guard duty!

Right after Rick was elected, our local newspaper asked if they could interview him regarding the issues that our county was facing. One issue they interviewed him about was water. They asked Rick question after question about what he would do to "regulate" water usage among home owners who owned their own wells and how he would prevent a drought in our county.

After patiently answering their many slanted questions, he added that God's system works well when we are wise with the resources. He pointed out that more surface water would help to recharge the aquifer and that even aquifer usage would eventually make its way back to the aquifer. Well, that one comment was all that the journalist needed in order to make Rick look like a right wing religious nut. The headlines read that *"Rep. Green says we should let God solve our water problems."*

The rest of the interview that they spent so much time on was hardly referenced throughout the article. That was our first bad experience with the press. We learned fast that it doesn't matter what you actually say because the journalist has the final word on how to portray everything you said. We also later learned to record every interview so that Rick could prove what he actually said.

Those are just some minor examples and ones that every elected official has to go through to some degree. During Rick's 3rd campaign in 2002, things became nasty and ugly, but not unheard of in the world of politics.

WHAT A MESS

Just a few weeks before the general election, we found out that the District Attorney's office in Austin began a criminal investigation against Rick based on a complaint filed by a liberal "watchdog group" that has mastered the art of causing havoc by filing complaints against elected officials right before an election in order to get the elected official bad press.

Rick is a lawyer, so the complaint filed against him alleged that he had represented a client in front of a state agency and did not sign in at the hearing as a lawyer instead of a state lawmaker. When Rick asked that the sign in sheets be shown to the DA to prove that he did sign in as a lawyer, the sign in sheets mysteriously couldn't be found by the state agency which is responsible for keeping those records.

Even worse, the video tape of Rick's testimony (wherein he clearly stated he was there for his client) also disappeared from this state agency. Even though the disappearance of information looked very suspect to us, the DA's office took the bait and worked hard to indict Rick right before the election in the fall of 2002.

To understand why Rick was targeted so much, you have to understand the shift of power that was going on at the time in Texas. The Democrats controlled the Texas House, but the Republicans were poised to win enough seats to take control of the House and elect a Republican Speaker.

The stakes were very high and unfortunately when so much power is on the line, you find out very fast who is willing to play ethically and who is willing to do whatever it takes to win. Rick was the incumbent but his district was a 50/50 district. Meaning, that it could swing Republican or Democrat based on who the candidate was and what was happening nationally.

All of the polls showed Rick winning with a big lead weeks before the election, but his race was the Democrat's #1 targeted race in the state. They wanted his seat back and they were willing to stop at nothing to get it back and they would spend as much money as it took.

The main newspaper from Austin ran terrible headlines on the front page talking about the investigation for ten days in a row during the last 2 weeks of the campaign. Although there was no meat to the investigation, all they needed was the headline that read *"Rep. Green under criminal investigation."* One of the journalists would later lose his job for collaborating with prosecutors on other stories and we still wonder to this day what kind of conversations were taking place between the newspaper, the prosecutors, and our opponent.

There was no way we could effectively counter the accusations in the last ten days of the campaign and undo the damage that the investigation and the media had done. For one, we didn't have enough time, and two, we didn't have enough money.

Rick will tell you today that he was naïve enough at the time to think people would not believe the accusations. But now he believes the old adage that if you tell a lie loud enough and long enough, it becomes truth to many people.

In the end, we were outspent 5 to 1 and the Democrats got their seat back by just a few hundred votes. Amazingly enough, after the election, the "investigation" that dominated every TV station and newspaper in most parts of Texas, just stopped.

Yes, that's right.

Vanished.

They didn't need an investigation anymore; they had beaten us at the polls by just a couple of hundred votes and that was their goal all along.

We now have an official letter from the new DA's office stating unequivocally that there was nothing to pursue and the file had been closed. Imagine that!

If you are wondering at all, I have a harder time than Rick forgetting the immense amount of emotional and physical worry and stress that went on during that time. He is much more willing to forget about the details and move on. I, on the other hand, have a harder time forgetting when someone accuses my husband of criminal activity.

I always wonder if God was testing us and toughening us up for something bigger down the road. I'm not sure what He has in store for us, but I now have an immense appreciation for the Christian men and women who are elected officials and have stuck to their values during all the trying times when it would be so much easier to just throw in the towel and give up.

Rick

ADMITTING MISTAKES

Lest you read the above and think I was always just the victim, now is a good time to own up to probably my biggest public arena mistake.

Though I admit to loving a good debate or political fight, I am not what you would call a physical brawler and have avoided physical confrontation most of my life.

I admit, however, that I tend to identify a bit with Peter in the New Testament and I just never can prevent the smile spreading across my face when I read about him taking out his sword and cutting off the ear of the man trying to arrest Jesus. I try to be more like Jesus, but sometimes I slip back into Peter mode, especially when someone comes after my family.

My confrontations have always been intellectual matches of wit in the courtroom, in the legislature, on the radio, or on the debate stage.

Except for one time.

Unfortunately, on this one occasion, I allowed the country boy side of me to decide how the conflict would be resolved.

First, a little more background is necessary.

Losing the 2002 campaign was a huge blessing in disguise for the Green family. I actually did not want to run again in 2002 and almost withdrew from the race just one week before the filing deadline. We even met with supporters and my pastor to tell them my heart was elsewhere and I was going to withdraw. I had an open door to speak for WallBuilders and learn at the feet of David Barton and I wanted to be able to coach Trey in baseball.

Unfortunately, my district was a top three race in the struggle over control of the Texas Legislature. If I didn't run, it was virtually guaranteed the Democrats would get the seat back and it would help them hold onto the majority in Texas.

If I did run, it was a tossup, but they would have to spend an awful lot of money to take the seat. I really wanted to see Republicans get the majority for the first time since Reconstruction because there were serious policies that had been killed for years by the Democrats. So in the final analysis, I had to run, but my heart just was not in it.

Had my opponent run an honest campaign, I would have easily dealt with him winning. After the election, I got to go fulfill my dream of coaching Trey and speaking nationally. The Democrats spent so much money on my race that it allowed Republicans to win some House seats they may not have otherwise won, thus allowing them to elect a Republican Speaker of the House.

A win/win for everyone!

However, the nastiness of the race made it very difficult to see the silver lining.

Earlier in this chapter, Kara gave you a small glimpse of the literal hell my family went through in the 2002 campaign. Kara said she has a harder time forgiving than me, but I readily admit that the taste of the 2002 campaign was something that was harder for me to overcome.

A good friend noticed that I was becoming bitter a few months later and gave me the book *Total Forgiveness*, by RT Kendal. I can honestly say that it helped me to root out any bitterness by radically changing my thinking and putting the race behind me. I point that out because despite the way news outlets, including Paul Harvey, reported the story I'm about to tell you, it truly was unrelated to the 2002 campaign. Had the story ended there, everyone would have been better off.

However, even though I was not on the ballot in 2004, my opponent from 2002 was running for re-election and He decided to run the same slanderous ads against me as a way of trying to hurt the candidate I was supporting.

We received phone call after phone call of people wondering if I was back in the race because the television ads talked more about me than the actual Republican candidate! Part of what bothered me the

most about these ads is that they took this picture of Trey and me from the house floor and blackened over his face.

Kara and I seriously considered a slander suit because the ads were beyond the pale in untruthfulness. But the standards for a public figure to win such a suit make it virtually impossible even when everything they are saying is proven false. We were really enjoying our life out of the political scene and decided it was not worth the time or money, so we just forgave again and moved on (well, maybe Kara didn't!).

AGAIN? YOU'VE GOT TO BE KIDDING!

I wish I had been able to be as forgiving the third time around when they did the same thing in 2006. This time it was one of those mailers with grainy pictures and complete lies and they even sent it to our family and neighbors.

We were just so amazed that even with me out of politics for four years, they would still drag our family name through the mud.

The mailer hit mailboxes the day before the election. When I saw my former opponent (who was responsible for all of these mailers) at the polls on Election Day, I should have just ignored him like the previous election.

If you're wondering if I had truly forgiven and let go of the past events, you should know that I had called my former opponent a few weeks earlier and offered my support to him if he chose to run for Congress against the ultra liberal holding that post. I specifically told him I was glad to bury the hatchet and work together for the good of the Country.

So the mailer really surprised me and I just had to ask him why he chose to keep dragging my family through the mud when I was no longer on the ballot and our previous phone conversation indicated we had opened a new chapter.

His response back to me was to laugh and say *"Your family doesn't mean s**t to me."*

After four years of ignoring him, he had finally pushed me over my limit.

It was the first real punch I had thrown since I was a kid, but it sent him to the ground.

It was wrong, foolish, and sinful. It set a horrible example for my children and for the young people in my community. I issued a public apology and to this day I wish I could go back and respond differently to his actions than I did.

Some would advise me to say nothing, but I'd rather just be honest and admit my mistakes than try to portray an image of perfection that just doesn't exist.

In most any other Texas town, that would have been the end of the story. But my former opponent and other political enemies saw an opportunity they thought would drive the nails into my political coffin (though one person called after the incident and said, "I thought in Texas it was a legitimate defense if the other guy *just needed hittin'*").

The opponent called the sheriff's office and gave a sworn affidavit to press charges for "serious bodily injury," while in the exact same hour he was scheduling as many television interviews as possible, including national programs like Fox News, claiming he dodged the punch and was never even hit.

Fortunately, his ego forced him to keep going on television saying he was never hit, which took the legs out from under the prosecution's case, and the charges were eventually dismissed.

I guess if I do ever run for office again, we will have a great slogan for the next campaign: *"He'll fight for Texas!"*

Kara

WHAT A SUPPORT TEAM!

The upside to running for office was that we met and became friends with some of the dearest people we've ever known.

Rita Steitle, Laurel Casas, Bruce Upham & his three boys campaigning at the polls

Some of our closest friends today came out of the many prayer groups that were in constant prayer for our family during Rick's time in office. We will always be so grateful for those who sent us encouraging notes, emails, and phone calls telling us to forge on and stay strong.

Our campaign prayer team

Although our political story sometimes seems unreal, I can't even begin to imagine what it must have been like for the men and their families who decided to commit treason against Great Britain and sign their names to the document that birthed our Freedom and gave us our Nation. They knew death was the price they would have to pay, and they were willing to do it for all the generations still to come.

We really have nothing to complain about – just a lot to learn. Those 56 men who signed the Declaration pledged their *"lives, fortunes, and sacred honor."* We are so fortunate that in today's America we don't have to die for being an elected official, and it is such a small sacrifice to pledge a little of our lives, a little of our fortunes, and a little of our sacred honor.

If you've ever considered running for office, I hope we haven't scared you off. I want to be as honest as possible, but I also want to convey that anything we went through is pale in comparison to what will happen if we take a back seat and stop being vigilant in protecting our liberties and restoring the moral bedrock that our country was clearly founded on. I can promise you that Rick and I will never back down from a political calling just because we don't want people to say bad things about us.

Over the years, we've encouraged many able men and women to run for office and if you know someone who would be a great candidate or if you are considering it yourself, I suggest that the first thing you do is get the full support of your spouse. You and your spouse need to be as one mind and share the same goals and expectations when exploring a run for office.

Seek advice from the people you trust and who will be brutally honest with you. Do your homework and find out what issues you need to learn more about. Find out what the Biblical Worldview is on issues that you are not sure about by using resources from WallBuilders (www.wallbuilders.com) and other pro family organizations.

If running for office is not your cup of tea, there are many other ways you can make a difference and impact the culture. Be sure and read Rick's book "Freedom's Frame" in which he lays out the principles that have made America successful and gives specific action steps we can all take to keep those principles alive.

Everyone's role does not have to be the same. I am personally more comfortable being behind the scenes and would never enjoy being the candidate. I am not in my comfort zone speaking to a group or being on a stage. I would rather do anything else than speak in public! I leave that part to my husband. If (please Lord don't make me) by any chance you ever see me on stage or speaking to an audience, I will declare right now that I am doing it against my will!

But anytime you see my kids or my husband on stage, rest assured I'm right behind the curtain cheering them on!

Everyone in my family is not that way. In fact, my father is a perfect example of an ordinary citizen stepping up to make a difference for the community.

My dad, Terry Kyle, was a union electrician for thirty years. Like many conservative union members, he was always frustrated with his union supporting liberal politicians against his will. For years, he had wanted to be more involved in government and serving the community. He would often sit down with Rick after Rick was in a debate and he'd say, *"When they said…you should have said…"*

Rick would always say, *"I'm the one with all the training and degrees, but your dad comes up with better responses than I could ever think of!"*

My dad earned a baseball and football scholarship to go to college, but when my grandfather died of a heart attack at only 44 years of age, my dad quit college and moved home in order to help take care of his mom and raise his four younger siblings. He never had the opportunity to go back to school and get his degree.

He has been a deacon in our church for twenty five years and has a God given gift of discernment in matters of conflict. In 2006, many in our community were looking for a good, honest, hard working candidate for Justice of the Peace and Dad was the perfect fit.

Dad & Rhett on the campaign trail

We jumped in and had a family campaign team once again with Dad winning in a landslide.

He was sworn into office in January of 2007 and proved once again that you do not have to have the perfect degree or large sums of money to make a difference in America.

The same goes for you and the people in your community. Whatever role God is calling you to fulfill...go do it and do it with joy!

It was a family celebration when Terry Kyle
was sworn in as Justice of the Peace.

**It is the duty of every good citizen to use all the
opportunities which occur to him, for preserving
documents relating to the history of our country.**

**Thomas Jefferson, letter to Hugh P. Taylor,
October 4, 1823**

PART III
BUS TRIPS AND BASEBALL

And whatsoever ye do, do it heartily, as to the Lord, and not unto men....

Colossians 3:23

OUR AMERICAN STORY

★

9

Kara

There is no such thing as the perfect bus. That is something we now know, but it was something we had to learn on our own. In 2003, we decided that we wanted to travel the nation with our kids. Rick was starting to speak nationally more often and we wanted to travel together as a family as much as we could, but we needed something that we could travel in that would be our home away from home.

We started the daunting task of researching RV's and buses. We literally did not know a thing about the "bus world" and soon

Big Bear, CA

became obsessed about learning and researching everything there was to know.

Our friends, Bruce and Holly Collie, introduced us to the world of "busing" as they traveled with their children (13 and counting as of this printing) when Bruce would speak. Bruce gave Rick a crash course in what to look for and passed along a box full of bus conversion magazines.

Rick ordered every other bus magazine there ever was and began reading everything he could get his hands on as I would search the many bus websites daily looking for that perfect bus for our family. There are some beautiful buses out there and once you see the million dollar ones, it's real hard to snap back to reality and remember that *"Oh yeah, that's a little out of our price range."*

Reagan, Kamryn, & Rhett making Hershey kisses in Hershey, PA

Eventually, we found a bus located in Texas that was within our price range and was once used as an entertainer bus by country singer Waylon Jennings. It also had bunk beds for the kids - that was a must for us. So after looking at a lot of pictures of it and asking a lot of questions, we finally set out to buy our new home away from home.

I can't say that I was jumping with joy when we first saw it. The interior was still from the 80's and there was a constant smell of smoke that was embedded in the walls and the fabric. When I cleaned the walls with a wet rag, the rag was instantly black from the smoke. Rick, ever the optimist, was looking at all the great things about it, while I was looking at my kids' red, watery eyes from the smell and wondering what in the world we had gotten ourselves into.

After we got home and I cleaned it the best I could, we took our first trip to Arkansas. Looking back now, I have to laugh at this first trip, although at the time I felt like driving the bus off a cliff! When we got to Arkansas where Rick was speaking, we noticed the air brakes were not working properly (Even I know that's not good!!).[i] We were in a little town, so

---

[i] **From Rick:** "Not working properly" is a bit of an understatement. One of the air brake chambers had been punctured by a broken spring. So as we would drive, the air tanks would empty faster than the compressor could keep them filled up. Air brakes on a big rig like this are purposefully designed to lock down when the air drops below a certain point...this way you are not going 60 mph down the highway and find out you have no brakes. So as the air would run out, the brakes would start locking down with us going down the road and I would pull over. As long as the brakes were locked down, the chamber with the leak was closed and the air tanks filled back up. So we'd sit on the side of the highway waiting for the tanks to fill up, then drive a few hundred yards until the air tanks got low and the brakes locked down, pull back over and wait for the tanks to fill up,

finding someone who knew anything about Eagle Buses was a chore in itself. We were finally able to get it to a mechanic. We rented a car, checked into a hotel, and waited. The next day we were headed back to Texas with working brakes.

It was in the middle of the summer (which means HOT) and this is when our AC unit decides that it doesn't want to blow cold air. It was blowing lukewarm air and was only coming out of one spot in the whole bus. Our kids were 8, 5, 4, and 1 years old at the time. All I

Yellowstone National Park

can remember doing for the whole drive from Arkansas to Texas was standing in the one spot where

---

get another few hundred yards down the road, etc., etc. until we finally made it to the shop. All the while I'm trying to convince Kara and the kids how great traveling in the bus is going to be!

you could feel air and taking turns holding each kid in front of the air vent so they wouldn't pass out from the heat! At the end of that trip, I was ready to sell the darn bus and forget traveling the nation. Thank goodness my husband didn't give up on the dream as easily as me. He pushed me to continue traveling.

In the meantime, though, Rick decided that the bus needed a whole make over. One morning he went into the bus just to check on one thing and by the afternoon, our front yard looked like a junk yard. He had started pulling out one piece of paneling to look behind it for a leak and ended up stripping out the entire inside of the bus! When I say entire, I mean all the way to the

The inside of the bus after Rick finished "checking on one thing."

steel beams, but the upside was that it didn't smell like smoke anymore!

After he stripped it to the beams, we stood in our front yard looking at a completely empty bus shell and then we looked at each other and said, *"Now what do we do?"*

LEARNING THE HARD WAY

Over the course of the next two years, Rick was forced to become an expert in anything that had to do with buses. He and Trey (who was only 9 at the time) re-built almost everything in the bus themselves. Rick insulated it, wired it, built the beds and cabinets, laid the floor, and installed the plumbing, not to mention a million other little things. [ii] We were fortunate enough to have

---

[ii] **From Rick:** I am the least mechanical guy in the world so this entire project was WAY outside my comfort zone. The worst part was that virtually everything I did on that bus, I did 2 or 3 or 4 times before I got it halfway right. I will admit there were some days I was pushed beyond my limits and wanted to give up and just burn the thing to the ground. Every time I was ready to quit, I just pictured the contrast of traveling alone in airport after airport versus being in that bus with my family by my side and that would push me on towards the finish line. Well, I should not say finish line since

OUR AMERICAN STORY

some good friends and family who also helped along the way and without whom we would have never made the first road trip in the new conversion.[iii]

Our dream was to have a road worthy home away from home that would allow us to be together fulfilling our mission and purpose as a family. Bruce warned Rick not to add up the receipts, but to just keep thinking about the family being together. But it's hard for a guy with a degree in Finance not to search out the bottom line. By the end of remodeling, our home on the road cost more than we had spent to build our little guest home in Dripping Springs!

---

there are still dozens of items on the "completion list" yet to be completed!

[iii] **From Rick:** We would have never had a road worthy bus if it had not been for the friends and family that helped. I remember several nights when Bruce Collie brought over a whole truckload of equipment and stayed out there working in that bus with me until 2:00 or 3:00 AM helping me get it ready for our first trip. Kara's dad, Terry Kyle, did the same thing on multiple occasions, even working with me to get last minute wiring done literally on the night we left for the maiden voyage of Lady Liberty (the name we gave to the new version of our bus).

We had never intended on remodeling a bus from scratch, but now that it's built the way we want it, we have enjoyed it so much over the last 5 years. The kids have their own bunk decorated like they wanted. It may not be a million dollar bus with all the bells and whistles, but the Lord has blessed us with a bus that has met our needs and allowed us to fulfill our purpose together.

Lady Liberty

We have traveled with the kids to 43 states and witnessed God's beautiful creation first-hand in places like Yellowstone National Park, Niagara Falls, Pikes Peak, and much more.

Niagara Falls

We tried a little fishing at Yellowstone, but the bear tracks scared us off pretty quick!

10

Kara

BEACHES & BANDAGES

Rick doesn't want me to write this chapter. He's afraid he will forever be known as the Clark Griswold of the speaking circuit. Remember the Griswolds and Chevy Chase from the *"Vacation"* series of movies?

Before we purchased and rebuilt our own bus, we rented RV's a couple of times to make sure we would enjoy this kind of traveling. While some of the mechanical work was being done on our bus during the new conversion, we rented an RV so we could go on a speaking tour with Rick to Florida and back. Of course, this was our chance to visit Disney as well.

On the way to Florida, Rick had a speaking engagement on the coast in Mississippi and we decided to take a couple of hours and enjoy the beach.

We had recently added a new member to our family, a little Tibetan Spaniel which Rick named *"Dutch."* President Ronald Reagan is Rick's political hero and President Reagan's nickname as a kid was Dutch. It wasn't enough for Rick to have one of his sons named Reagan and another son born on Ronald Reagan's birthday...he even named the dog after the president! He also tried to convince me to name a child *"Thatcher"* after Margaret Thatcher, but I had to draw the line somewhere.

Back to the beach....We parked, got everyone out of the RV, and then tied Dutch's leash to the back of the RV so he wouldn't get loose and get lost. Now, before you let your imagination think the worst, please read ahead…

As is too often the case, we stayed too long and were running late to Rick's speaking engagement. Somehow in the chaos of washing 6 pairs of sandy feet and changing clothes, everyone in our family walked right past poor little Dutch and no one loaded him in the RV.

Fortunately, Dutch's fate was not the same as the dog in "Vacation." We had just pulled away from the curb and gone about 50 feet down the street and were crossing over into the left hand turn lane when a car swerved around us honking and hanging out the window to tell us about the dog that we were (gulp) dragging. All of our hearts leapt into our throats as Rick slammed on the breaks in the middle of the road and rushed out the door of the RV to what we thought would be a horrific sight.

That must have been the fastest little Spaniel in history because he managed to keep up with us most of the way and skid the rest of the way without incurring any real damage to his body.

The pads on his little feet, however, were burned just about all the way off. Rick was cuddling him like an infant child when he came back into the

bus and we were all in tears as we looked at his poor little feet. We rushed to a nearby vet and got the little guy bandaged up. He had a cast put on each leg

Dutch gets the royal treatment from Reagan

that went all the way up to his shoulders. He had to lie on the couch with all four legs sticking straight out for days before he could walk. The worst part was that we had to stop at a new vet every other day to get his bandages changed during the rest of the trip. We spent more money on Dutch during that trip than we've spent on all of our other animals combined. Yes, it was guilt money...Rick said he would pay whatever it took because he felt so bad.

You might be wondering where little Dutch is today. Well, after all the tears and money and searching for vets, we got back home to the ranch in Dripping Springs with Dutch just about completely healed up. Two weeks later he was sleeping under my uncle's big F250 pickup truck and must have been in a really deep sleep, because he didn't hear that very loud truck start. Well, you can figure out the rest, but needless to say, we've decided not to name any more dogs after presidents.

Rick

Now that I am on the ten most hated list of every PETA (the radical "People for the Ethical

Treatment of Animals") member in the world (thanks Kara!)...can we talk about something else?

HIGHWAY ANGELS AND MECHANICS

I have not yet met a bus owner who was without a few breakdown stories. One of the first times I had the chance to visit with Jim Bob Duggar (He and his wife, Michelle, and their 18 children are an AMAZING family), we hit it off trading breakdown stories. Even the Prevost (much nicer and more expensive than our Eagle) owners have problems on the road once in awhile...it's just part of the deal when you decide to haul an entire house around with you at 65 miles per hour!

We've had some quick fix breakdowns and some serious ones that had us stranded for multiple days. But the one thing I remember the most about our breakdowns is that in every single case, without exception, God has protected us from injury and has placed us in good hands with mechanics who took great care of us.

One of my greatest fears of traveling in a bus is that my lack of mechanical knowledge would allow us to be taken advantage of by a mechanic when we broke down in small towns. If they knew that I did not know much about the big rig parts and they knew I wanted to get down the road, it would be easy for me to get gouged on the pricing.

Not once has such a thing happened. In fact, the exact opposite has occurred. Every single time we

In front of the Mayflower II

have had a breakdown, we have met hard-working, great Americans who went out of their way to save us money and get us back on the road as quickly as possible. What could have been extremely negative experiences turned into positive experiences meeting neat people and being blessed by their expertise, craftsmanship, and professionalism. From big cities like Los Angeles, Nashville and New York, to small towns in Arkansas,

Kentucky, and Texas, we have been treated wonderfully by our fellow Americans.

HISTORY UP CLOSE

It is one thing to read about a battlefield in a textbook. It is completely another to stand in the place where it happened or drive through the entire battlefield with sound effects and the story being told. We've been able to visit Gettysburg, Vicksburg, Valley Forge, Lexington, and so many other places where historic battles took place.

At Lexington, MA where the shot heard 'round the world' was fired. Pastor Garret Lear brought the history to life for

We've seen all of these places together as a family, but one of my favorite memories of a battlefield was with only Trey when we stayed at the

"Battlefield Bed & Breakfast" literally on the Gettysburg battlefield. It is an 1809 farm house that survived the battle. They kept us up late with ghost stories, served a hearty breakfast, and then took us out to shoot muskets. Trey didn't like the ghost stories, but he sure liked shooting that musket!

Vicksburg Battlefield re-enactment

It is much easier to appreciate and remember the sacrifices of previous generations when you see it firsthand. We strongly urge you that when you plan your vacations, do more than just water parks and Disney. Take time for some history that your children will remember forever.

PATRICK HENRY IN PERSON

That brings me to probably my very favorite historical location we have visited...Williamsburg, VA. It is certainly the best bang for the buck because you will see Jamestown, Yorktown, and Williamsburg all three in one trip.

James Fort in
Jamestown, VA

The best part was Colonial Williamsburg. You literally step back in time to the buildings, the characters, the costumes and all. Men, women, and children are playing the parts of some of our most famous and important patriots and they stay in character the entire time.

Our kids join the patriot
march to the Capitol

Since I often give bits and pieces of Patrick Henry's famous *"Give me Liberty or give me death"* speech, I was on a mission to find him and get a chance to hear at least part of that speech. He gave that speech on my birthday, March 23, 1775 at St. Johns Church in Richmond, so the actual re-enactment does not take place at Colonial Williamsburg. But I thought the man playing his character might be willing to play along and feed my need for some of the most famous patriotic words in our history.

Those early Colonists had a very effective way to put a kid in time out!

At one point in the day, he was taking questions from the audience just outside the Capitol building. They treat you like you are part of the townspeople of 1775, so you do your best to get in character as well. When called upon, I asked *"Mr.*

Henry, I too wish to throw off the chains of despotism, but how could we possibly win against a force so strong when even our own people say we are too weak."

The gentleman playing Patrick Henry needed no further nudging; he was a real pro and immediately said (almost word for word from the original speech):

"Yes, yes. They tell us, sir, that we are weak— unable to cope with so formidable an adversary. But when shall we be stronger? Will it be next week, or next year? Will it be when we are totally disarmed and when a British guard shall be stationed in every house? Shall we gather strength by irresolution and inaction? . . . Sir, we are not weak if we make a proper use of those means which the God of nature hath placed in our  *power. Three millions of people armed in the holy cause of liberty and in such a country as that which we possess are invincible by any force which our enemy can send against*

us. Besides, sir, we shall not fight our battles alone. There is a just God who presides over the destinies of nations and who will raise up friends to fight our battles for us. The battle, sir, is not to the strong alone; it is to the vigilant, the active, the brave. Gentlemen may cry peace, peace—but there is no peace! The war is actually begun! The next gale that sweeps from the north will bring to our ears the clash of resounding arms! Our brethren are already in the field! Why stand we here idle? What is it that gentlemen wish? What would they have? Is life so dear, or peace so sweet as to be purchased at the price of chains and slavery? Forbid it, Almighty God! I know not what course others may take; but as for me, give me liberty or give me death!!!"

You could have knocked me over with a feather. My trip was complete. For a student of history like me that is also a patriot, it was a moment I will never forget.

Later in the day, we ran into Mr. Henry when he was just walking down the street and he showed the boys how his cane was really a sword...they still talk about it to this day!

Trey & Reagan learning firsthand about the victory at Yorktown

FAVORITE BUS TRIPS

Kara

One fun thing we started doing was to collect a

key chain from every neat place we visit. We've got key chains from all over the United States and the collection has grown into a huge mass of clanking metal!

Kamryn, Reagan, & Trey at The Hermitage, the home of President Andrew Jackson

We have so many good memories, but there

are some that stand out as our favorites. The one that tops the list by far is the trip to the Reagan Ranch in Santa Monica, CA, in 2005. The ranch is not open to the public, but we happen to have a very good friend, Norma Zimdahl, who was able to set up a private tour of the ranch for us. In order to get to there, you have to drive up a very windy road to the top of this tall mountain. Once we got out and started walking around, our Reagan noticed the sign on the front gate that said "Reagan Ranch" and he got a big smile on his face and said, *"Cool, is the whole place for me?"* (he gets his optimism from his dad)

We were in such awe as we walked through the home that they had loved with all their heart. When Mrs. Reagan sold it to the foundation that now owns it, she left virtually everything in it just as it was when they lived there. Even their Bibles were left on the dresser open to each of their favorite versus.

We also got to walk through President Reagan's shed with all of his tools, chainsaws, and knick knacks still in their place.

What you wouldn't believe the most about the ranch house, is how simplistic it was. There was nothing fancy about it at all. In fact, it's been said that visiting dignitaries often commented that it was not fit for a President to live in. There was nothing pretentious about it and I think that it was very reflective of President Reagan's personality. He was confident in who he was and didn't need to prove his position of power by living in a home that didn't suit him. As long as he had his wife and his horses, he was a happy man.

This is the entrance to the house on the Reagan Ranch. It was a very simple home. We are with Rick's parents and nephews Kyle & Austin.

I think the American people trusted him as our President because of his genuine love for our Country that came through in his actions and his words. Seeing how simple he lived, when he could have lived in anything he wanted, really made me appreciate even more that he was our President.

I'm not the emotional one in the family (Rick is!), but gosh darn, it brings tears to my eyes when I think about how much our Country needs another Reagan - someone who inspires the type of Patriotism that our Founding Fathers taught about. It so saddens me to think that our current President has apologized to the world for America's mistakes more than he has edified her. That is why it is up to you and me to teach Patriotism to our kids.

When President Reagan died, our TV stayed on Fox News that whole week as we remembered this great man. The kids and I watched the Washington, DC ceremonies on TV while Rick and his dad attended in person (his account of that trip is in Appendix A). We knew we probably had the kids on "Reagan overload" when one morning Kamryn (3 years old at the time) announced to her brothers that

Ronald Reagan had died on the cross for our sins! Apparently, our morning Bible devotion and our admiration for Reagan were getting a little mixed up!

WE DIDN'T JUST DO THAT!

A couple of years ago, we traveled up the East Coast all the way into Canada, Massachusetts, Rhode Island, and New York. On our journey through New York, we were headed to Jersey City to an RV park that was right on the harbor across from the Statue of Liberty. When you drive a 40' long bus anywhere, not to mention New York City, it can get dangerous at times and you can easily get yourself into a position that is hard to get out of.

Well, we didn't plan very well when we started driving from upper Manhattan and drove 100 blocks through NYC!! If you've ever driven through NYC in a car, you know how crazy it is! Well magnify that by 100 times and that can somewhat describe how nerve racking it was to drive with everyone laying on their horns all around you, giving you the finger, and yelling expletives!

First of all, our bus almost took up two lanes and then when you add the crazy driving that goes on there, we were constantly slamming on our brakes trying to avoid a collision, which added to every New Yorkers frustration behind us!

It was such an eye opening experience and made us appreciate the wide open spaces of the South. Rick took it all in stride and throughout the whole drive of 100 blocks, he just smiled and waved to everyone and kept saying in his best hick accent, *"Howdy! We're from Texas!"*

It doesn't end there! When we got to the underground tunnel that connected us to Jersey City, we panicked for a moment and thought that our bus was too tall for the tunnel. We had to pull over (which is impossible in NYC), get out, and measure the height of the bus with a measuring tape and a ladder. Yeah, we're dorks! Traffic was stopped behind us, and let's just say that's the last time Lady Liberty will ever see downtown New York! We couldn't get an accurate measurement because we were using a flimsy measuring tape, so we just decided to go for it and if we took off our AC units on the top of the bus, it was worth it to get out of the city! Needless to say, we made it free and clear through the tunnel and we actually enjoyed the rest of the trip!

Crossing the Brooklyn Bridge on foot

★

11

Rick

There is just something about baseball. If you get chills at a game when they play the National Anthem or when a home run is hit and they play the theme music from *"The Natural"* or you still rank *"Field of Dreams"* in the top ten movies of all time, then you know what I mean.

One of my favorite movie lines ever is from *"The Final Season"* when the retiring coach tells the kid he is trying to convince to come back to the small town and take over as head coach, *"Remember kid, baseball is the only game where the object is to get home."*

I could watch *"The Rookie," "Major League," "Eight Men Out," "The Final Season," "For Love of the Game,"* and even *"A League of Their Own"*[iv] a hundred times each and I'd still be excited about each pitch despite already knowing the outcome.

Reagan shows off the ball Aaron Hill, 2nd baseman for the Toronto Blue Jays, threw to him between innings at Oriole Park at Camden Yards in Baltimore

---

[iv] Unfortunately, almost none of these movies should be watched without ClearPlay or some other method of cleaning up the movie. We usually get our movies from Hollygood Films because they do a great job of taking out the bad language and anything else inappropriate for the kids.

A Family Quest

I'm sure that traveling families better than ours set lofty educational goals like visiting science museums and art galleries. While we do try to see presidential museums and birthplaces, as well as battlefields and even burial places for Signers of the Declaration of Independence, our family's number one travel goal is to watch a game at all 30 Major League Baseball Parks.

Trey & I enjoy a Rangers game in 2009 where Hank Blaylock hit a walk off home run in extra innings.

Four years ago Trey was on a speaking trip with me in Colorado. We rode horses in the mountains, went up to the top of Pike's Peak, saw the Garden of the God's, and watched a Colorado Rockies game at Coors Field. At some point in the game Trey said it would be neat to see all the different stadiums and our quest was born!

Atlanta Braves in 2006

We have now been to 21 stadiums, including the old Yankee Stadium, which means we'll end up visiting a total of 31 after we go to the new Yankee Stadium.

These days when I get a speaking request for any date between April and October, the first thing I do is check the MLB schedule in their area then I consider all the other factors!

We've had great seats right behind home plate or the base paths and we've sat in the nose bleed sections of several parks. We've had the chance to do tours of dugouts and locker rooms, batting cages and press boxes. We always have peanuts, hot dogs, and nachos and we never leave without a pennant to hang on the boys' wall.

On our tour of the Kansas City Royals' Kauffman Stadium the kids got to hold their own pre-game press conference (well, sort of!)

Arizona Diamondbacks in 2006

JUST ONE PITCH

Our only rule for a stadium trip to count is that we have to see at least one official pitch. Most of the time we see the whole game, but once in awhile we get their late or have to leave early.

On one occasion, we barely were able to record the visit. Trey and I were on a speaking trip in Pittsburgh, Pennsylvania with no plans to see a game because we were booked every night to speak. Then we happen to drive by PNC Park on the way to our engagement. The cars were lined up for the game and the lit up marquee was advertising the night's game.

Like moths to a flame, we could not resist. I told Trey I'd talk even faster than normal in my speech and we'd try to catch the last couple of innings if we could get tickets.

More people wanted to visit after the speech than we had expected, so we were cutting it close as we drove to the park. We listened to the game on the radio and since the Pirates were up by so many runs, we knew there may not be a bottom of the 9th so we were running out of time.

Anaheim Angels in 2006

Toronto Blue Jays' Rogers Centre in 2007

Fortunately we got a parking spot very close to an entrance and took off running as the 9th inning was beginning. People were already leaving the game so we asked a group of people if we could have two of their tickets so we could see just one pitch. Two guys said sure and we sprinted for the gate only to be told the tickets could not be used for re-entry and we would need to go to the ticket window and purchase tickets. I told the guy about our goal of seeing at least one pitch at each stadium and that we didn't have time to find the ticket window, but he was having none of the dream and waived me off.

We sprinted to the ticket window and by this time, I'm sure nine year old Trey was wondering why he ever mentioned the idea of seeing all the stadiums. The guy at the ticket window was curious about why I was buying tickets with only an out or two left in the game. When I quickly explained, he gave me two tickets for free. We ran through the gate handing off our tickets and sprinted up the ramp to find ourselves at the Left Field corner and literally arrived as the pitcher was delivering his pitch with two outs.

The batter grounded out to first.

Game Over.

We saw one pitch. We were so out of breath we had to stand there and rest while the rest of the fans filed out of the stadium. Crazy! But there is just something about baseball!

Well, we got the pennant and saw the pitch, but no hot dog, peanuts, or nachos. Such a travesty had to be corrected and just a few weeks before this book went to print we were blessed by our friends Bob and Peep Scheidemantel with a full game at PNC that included all the fixins!

Sometimes my pace is a little too crazy for everyone else. I had a couple of speaking requests in the northeast and thought it would be fun to have a generational baseball trip with my sons and their grandfathers. So I booked flights and bought baseball tickets for my dad, Kara's dad, Trey, Reagan, and me.

Sounds like a wonderful bonding experience, right? Well, did I forget to mention that I like to squeeze as much into as little time as possible?

Three Major League Baseball games at three different stadiums in 24 hours!

What? Why is that overdoing it?

We saw the Mets in New York for a Noon game on Wednesday, then the Philadelphia Phillies at home that evening at 7:05 PM, then the Washington Nationals at home the next day at 1:05 PM.

We even squeezed in a trip to Independence Hall and saw the Liberty Bell

Let's avoid the details and just say that Kara's dad is pretty sure he never wants to travel with me again. The best part of the trip was my dad getting absolutely chewed out by a New York policewoman because he accidentally ended up in the toll tag line instead of the cash line when we were crossing the Verrazano Bridge...but that's a whole different story!

Busch Stadium for the St. Louis Cardinals in 2009

WITNESSING HISTORY

We have had the chance to witness firsthand some of baseball's great moments. We've seen walk off home runs, come from behind story book wins, and grand slams. We were able to see Roger Clemens first game back with the Astros when he came out of retirement and we were at AT&T Park for Barry Bonds' home run #761.

Probably the most exciting and historic game we attended was the San Diego Padres when Trevor Hoffman got his 500th Save. For the less than die hard baseball fans, this is like seeing Nolan Ryan's 5,000th strikeout. That was an absolutely electric evening. I've never heard a stadium go so crazy. We were sitting next to a true baseball fan from Philadelphia. With that Philly accent that makes baseball even better, he was telling us in the 7th inning that if the Padres were ahead by less than four runs after the bottom of the 8th, then we were going to get to see history.

Trey & I had great seats for the Oakland A's in 2008

The 8th Inning ended and it suddenly felt like a heavy metal concert. The speakers began blaring the song *"Hell's Bells,"* by ACDC, which begins with loud church bells, and all the large screens started flashing *"Trevor Time."* Just as the guitar and drums started, the Center Field wall opened up and out ran Trevor Hoffman. The place absolutely erupted. Needless to say, he finished off the Dodgers and history was made. They even stamped our tickets with *"Trevor Time – 500."*

Now, I'm not into hero worship of a man, but I do very much enjoy historic moments and that was a fun one.

We happened to be at the Texas Rangers game in June of 2009 when they hosted the Houston Astros and Ivan "Pudge" Rodriguez, Trey's favorite player[v], for an historic evening.

That night Pudge made history by catching his 2,227[th] game, breaking the record set by Hall of Famer Carlton Fisk. About midway through the game, the announcer paused the game and pointed out the history to the crowd. We came to our feet and cheered for what seemed like a full five minutes.

---

[v] Actually, it's a tie between Pudge and Josh Hamilton for both Trey and me. So the Rangers getting Pudge back for the last part of the 2009 Season has made it a double thrill for us to watch our team play!

We were sitting right behind the 3rd base dugout when Pudge took off his mask and waived to the crowd. Grown men, including this one, were tearing up over what a non-baseball fan might call *"just another game."*

But that's because they do not know the history.

The Green's are joined by friends and fellow ballplayers Matt, Parker, & Sawyer Patterson at Rangers Ballpark for Pudge's record breaking night. We finally managed to get Kara in one of these photos since she was not behind the camera!

Pudge started his career with us. Just as my baseball playing days were ending at the age of 20, I was watching him become the youngest catcher in the Major Leagues at only 19. His debut, literally on the same day as his wedding, was June 20, 1991. His grit and hustle and hard work made him one of the most popular players in Ranger history.

Ironically (or better said...just part of the baseball magic), the opposing catcher that day Pudge debuted in the Majors was none other than Carlton Fisk. And in 1993 when Fisk set the record of most games caught at 2,226, can you guess who the opposing catcher was? Yep, Pudge Rodriguez.

You might say *"big deal"* and I admit that I can't really explain why these many coincidences and nuances are such a special part of the game.

I've tried to figure out what makes baseball so special in America and I still can't put my finger on it, but I do have some theories.

Maybe we're just living out our dreams through others. Maybe we're just admiring someone able to do something we only dreamed of doing. Maybe it's recognizing part of the beauty of the game is that brute strength or speed is not enough. It really is a game of multiple skills. To play it well requires a certain amount of grace, focus, smarts, composure, and, yes...luck.

It's the excitement of the unknown because anything can happen in baseball. We keep all the stats and records, knowing full well that the most exciting moments are those that defy the odds and the numbers. We love to see a Perfect Game[vi] because it is like defying gravity, it just seems scientifically and physically impossible. More common are those moments when a guy comes off the bench and gets the big hit or makes the big play.

Whether in the pros or in little league, we love to see the underdog win.

Maybe that's why baseball is so naturally tied to American patriotism. Because the little guy, the scrappy team, the unexpected hero...they all get a chance. And it's not just once in awhile, but every day on baseball fields all across America, that some kid's dream comes true. Maybe he doesn't set an MLB record or get inducted to the Hall of Fame, but for one moment in time he gets to make the play he'll remember for his entire life. And for the fan, it's enough to just witness that small piece of history.

[vi] A Perfect Game is when no runner on the opposing team reaches base safely for the entire game.

Texas Rangers Ballpark at Arlington

12

Rick

Reagan, Rick, Rhett, & Trey when Trey hit his first homerun

I think maybe that opportunity for lifetime memories and lessons we talked about in the last chapter is why I enjoy coaching kids in baseball. It use to be simply about spending time with my own boys and that is still the main reason I spend so much time with youth baseball.

But I've recently found another reason and benefit to coaching...for love of the game. To be more accurate, it's not actually love of the game, but a love of what the game does for the kids. I have found youth baseball to be the most effective outlet for teaching life lessons to young boys becoming men. It

I always tell parents that if they don't want me praying with their boys, it's the wrong team for them! Even little Rhett got in on the action in this post-game prayer.

works the same with any sport, but in the Green family, it happens to be baseball.

They learn that hard work pays off, team is more important than me, sometimes things just don't go your way and the important thing is how you respond to them, attitude is just as important as aptitude, and so many other lessons.

Dad & Reagan

I have so much to learn about coaching baseball. I am not an expert on the rules or the skills and often have to ask an umpire to explain something for me. I'm always calling friends who are more experienced coaches for advice.

I'm very competitive, and when I first started coaching my boys I was way too worried about the score for their age of play. Once in awhile I became like those parents that make the other kids and players want to find another sport!

My prayer is that as I am getting older and more experienced, the game is in much better perspective and my actions are a better example to the players! These days if I feel my passion getting the better of me, I just look over at Kara in the stands and she gives me that *"don't even think about it Mister"* look and then I remember the real reason we're on the field in the first place.

Pre-game pep talk!

I have two major themes I use throughout the season.

GIVING YOUR BEST

The first comes from Colossians 3:23:

"And whatever you do, <u>do it heartily</u>, as to the Lord and not to men..."

Other versions say things like *"diligently"* or *"put your heart into it"* or *"work willingly"* or *"with all your heart"* or *"the best that you can."*

We teach our players to give it their best every time they swing the bat, throw the ball, run the bases, make a catch, and so on. But it is not just when you're the guy at the plate or the one to whom the ball has been hit. The verse says *"whatever you do"* so that applies when you're on the bench and cheering your teammates, or when you're warming up the left fielder, or you're shagging baseballs at practice, or you're cleaning your room, or doing your chores, or your school work, and on and on.

Reagan ready to fire

Two things missing among too many youth today are passion and purpose. Unless they are the star and the center of attention, they see no need to give their best. As Christians, we can teach our children that such an attitude is disobedience to God's Word and therefore it is sin. But even to the kid on the team that is not a Christian, you can still teach the practical benefits of approaching everything in life with zeal and joy and passion. You can point out the difference in their results both on and off the field when they give it their best every single time.

Trey works very hard to play the game at his best

The kids figure out pretty quick that the best reward is not the *"results"* on the field in terms of stats like home runs and double plays; it is the personal satisfaction that you really gave your absolute best...regardless of the results, that you held nothing back, left it all on the field, and that you really did play *"with all your heart."*

The most important part is found in the rest of the verse... *"as to the Lord and not to men."* I attempt to teach our boys that if they are trying to perform for mom and dad, or the fans, or for us coaches, then their joy and satisfaction will be dependent upon the ups and downs of the game and they will live an emotional roller coaster. But if they are doing their best as to the Lord, do they really think God is mad or disappointed when they make an error or strike out? It is so much easier to wipe away a mistake and give your best on the next play when you are not worried about impressing or disappointing "men."

This is not at all to say one should take a lazy *"no big deal, I don't care"* approach to the game or anything else in life. Such blandness is exactly the opposite of the first part of the verse we already discussed. I have yet to meet a person whose *"best"* is reflected in such an attitude that is clearly not *"heartily"* or *"diligent."*

REAL MEN RALE

The second major theme came from the suggestion of one of my fellow coaches, James Beach. He had an outstanding suggestion that became sort of a team motivator before each game. He and I both had been implementing the book *"Raising a Modern Day Knight,"* by Robert Lewis, with our oldest boys. In the book, Lewis lays out the acronym RALE and says that real men:

Reject Passivity

Accept Responsibility

Lead Courageously

Expect God's Reward

Just imagine all the coaching opportunities in those four items and how they can apply to the game...but more importantly to life!

Rejecting passivity means charging the baseball, aggressively going after the ball, being the one to jump in and clean the dugout, stepping up at the plate with a purpose in mind, being mentally in the game and ready to pounce on opportunities to steal bases or make a play.

Rhett making a play

Accepting responsibility means not blaming the glove or a bad hop or a teammate or the coach or your parents or your 1st grade teacher. It means simply saying *"my bad"* and immediately jumping back in and trying even harder on the next play. It means aggressively calling that fly ball that is in your territory. It means practicing on your own at home without someone having to tell you. It means keeping up with your equipment and not blaming your mom if your glove is not in your bag!

Leading courageously is somewhat the opposite of rejecting passivity, but it is also a chance to point out courage is not the absence of fear, but the overcoming of that fear. I also remind the boys that the Lord has not given us a spirit of fear, but of power, love, and a sound mind (2 Timothy 1:7). Sound mind means no wavering, no wondering if the ball is going to hit me in the mouth, no thinking about the negatives, totally focused on the desired outcome

Servant leadership & leading by example can be learned on the field

and confident. If I have a player that is afraid of the ball, then I have them repeat *"power, love, and a sound mind"* every time I hit them a grounder and every time they step into the batter's box.

Expecting God's reward does not mean winning a baseball game or getting a job promotion. I teach the boys that God's reward is the joy they get from playing the game the best that they can, from building relationships with their teammates, and from honoring God in their actions and attitude.

Don't get me wrong, I don't like to lose...at anything! So my teams are very competitive. We play to win and often do so! However, it is so important to teach them that winning is a byproduct of the real reward.

The best part of T-ball is snacks after the game! Rhett is on the right, cousins Shel & Luke on the left

COOPERSTOWN DREAMS PARK

This past baseball season, our team played in the most amazing youth sporting event I've had the privilege of being a part of.

We were one of one hundred and three teams staying at what I came to call *"baseball heaven"* in the beautiful Catskill Mountains of upstate New York where baseball was invented in 1839. Twenty-Two immaculate, perfectly cut youth baseball fields and a bunkhouse for each team...just imagine the possibilities.

That's exactly what the Presutti family did and they turned their imagination into reality.

Lou Presutti's father had once said that every kid in America should have the chance to play in Cooperstown and Lou has since made that dream a reality for thousands of kids each summer.

Lou told us at the beginning of the tournament that the kids were going to get to live the dream, making plays and hits they had never done before. He was 110% correct. Every kid on our team left Cooperstown with a lifelong memory of an amazing catch, hit, play, or pitching performance they had the opportunity to be a part of.

I want to thank Lou for making the dream a reality. And special thanks to the families associated with our team for giving me the best coaching experience of my life!

If your kids are playing youth baseball, plan to take a team to Cooperstown in their 12 year old season and you will make a lifetime of memories.

The Green kids & some of Trey's teammates get a picture with Lou Presutti & thank him for making the dream come true.

From left to right: Caleb Beach, Reagan, Trey, Leighton Klepac, Lou Presutti, Kamryn, Rhett, & Addison Denslow

PART IV
DOING YOUR PART

Render Honor to Whom Honor Is Due

Romans 13:7

OUR AMERICAN STORY

TEACH YOUR KIDS TO HONOR OUR VETERANS

★

13

Rick

If you ever have a problem getting fired up about the importance of preserving the greatness of our nation, just go to your local VFW hall, sit with some of those veterans, and listen to their stories.

In fact, if you have kids or grandkids, take them with you and involve them in the conversation. Make it a mission in life to ingrain in your kids and grandkids the sacrifices those men and women made in order for us to enjoy the freedoms we enjoy today. One of the most important legacies we can leave our kids is equipping them with an unbridled passion for defending America.

As long as I can remember, I have had a pride and admiration for our armed service men and women. It was something that was instilled in me early on and something Kara and I hope to pass on to our kids. Before Trey was even old enough to walk, I made it a point to take him with me anytime we saw a soldier - whether we were at a restaurant, the grocery store, or the airport - and I would go up to the soldier, shake their hand, and tell them *"Thank you for your service."*

Now that they are a little older, when we see a soldier, all four of our kids practically take off running just to shake their hand and thank them.

We have had all kinds of responses. Some soldiers are very humbled and quiet, some return the thank you with a big smile and high five, and some seem a little overwhelmed with four kids running up to them with a lot of enthusiasm!

Every time it has been such a blessing to Kara and I to know that with every hand shake, our kids are looking up to that soldier with heroic admiration because they know what those soldiers do for our country.

This picture is of me, Kamryn, and Rhett with our good friend, retired Lt. Col. Brian Birdwell. He was the closest survivor at the point of impact at the Pentagon on 9/11. The majority of his body was burned and his story is incredible to read. He is the author of the book *"Refined by Fire."*

Not too long ago our family was on a bus trip and we had to stop in Nashville to have some tires looked at on our bus. When you are in Nashville, you cannot go wrong when looking for a good mechanic who can work on buses. We stopped at one of the best bus shops you could ask for and we all piled out and headed to the customer lounge to wait.

While we were in there waiting, an 88 year old man walked in with a big smile and introduced himself as the owner of the place. He looked much younger than his age and as soon as he found out that we were huge baseball fans, he sat down and talked baseball and politics with us for two hours.

During the conversation, he brought up that he had fought in WWII. Upon hearing that, our kids sat up a little straighter and started paying a little more attention to what he was saying. When there was a break in the conversation, each one of the kids walked over to him, shook his hand, and thanked him for his service.

His response is something I will never forget. He lowered his head a little and blushed from all the attention, then he said, *"Thanks, but I feel like I don't deserve all that. I don't think I contributed much."* Wow. His humility was so genuine and that is what makes his generation one of the greatest ever.

As a society, we are cheating this generation of kids by not seeking out more ways to let them interact with veterans. One day, the WWII generation will have passed away and all we will have are stories passed down.

That is why we have taught our kids about their great-grandfather (Kara's grandfather) earning his purple heart at Iwo Jima during WWII. When I was in the Legislature, I passed a resolution honoring his life and listed all of the different places he had fought during the war. We have the resolution hanging up in our house today. Even though the kids never knew him, they are proud to tell people about his role in securing freedom for our Nation.

Our family is also privileged to know many of the veterans in our hometown. When we held our big campaign fundraisers every year, we would have a huge showing of veterans, which was such an honor to us. My favorite part of the evening was recognizing them.

If you haven't already gotten to know your local vets, then start today. Make it a priority. You'll be greatly blessed by it and you will greatly bless that soldier or veteran by taking the time to listen to them.

Most importantly, it will teach your kids more than any book ever can.

Rick's most prized award is the Legislative Vanguard Award given to him by the Non Commissioned Officers Association for passage of HB 1776, The Teach Freedom Act. Pictured here is VFW Post Commander Gary Hale presenting Rick with the local veterans' appreciation award as well.

The Green's with American Heroes
Shorty & Jimmy Barnett

14

Rick

In 1788, Noah Webster said:

Every child in America should be acquainted with his own country. He should read books that furnish him with ideas that will be useful to him in life and practice. As soon as he opens his lips, he should rehearse the history of his own country.

It does not get much clearer than that. It is our responsibility to teach our kids what the founders intended for every American to know. Leaving it up to the schools (public or private either one) or to their college education is a huge mistake with generational ramifications.

Trey became a huge fan of Gov. Mike Huckabee during the 2008 Presidential election. He had broken his arm and managed to get the Gov to sign the cast at his last big rally of the campaign.

Trust me, there are plenty of parents out there who are doing the opposite. They are teaching their kids there is no right and wrong and there is no God, or that America really is not that special of a place.

Our job is to equip our youth with the right Biblical worldview so they can go toe to toe with the ones who are being brought up to condemn America and everything she stands for.

So that means we must teach them the truth *and* teach them how to articulate and defend that truth.

That is why I started Patriot Academy[vii] eight years ago, but Patriotism must first begin in our homes. We must make it a priority to not only teach Patriotism in our home, but also to live it.

We often hear that our children learn more from what we do than from what we say. This is also true with the way we exercise our freedoms and participate in our stewardship government.

[vii] Patriot Academy is a one week youth leadership program we hold at the Texas State Capitol for 16 to 25 year olds from all across America. As they live the life of a legislator, the students learn a Biblical worldview of government, the process of the legislature, and the skills necessary to be effective leaders in whatever area of the culture to which God has called them.

"Patriotism is as much a virtue as justice, and is as necessary for the support of societies as natural affection is for the support of families."

—Benjamin Rush

Signer of the Declaration of Independence

How true those words are. Instilling Patriotism in our children is what will sustain our country for generations to come. Without it, there is no reason to believe that America will continue to thrive or be the example to the world that she has been.

You can start today by teaching your children the heart of the Declaration of Independence we discussed in Chapter 7:

We hold these truths to be self-evident, that all men are created equal, that they are endowed by their Creator with certain unalienable Rights, that among these are Life, Liberty and the pursuit of Happiness. That to

secure these rights, Governments are instituted among Men, deriving their just powers from the consent of the governed.

Kara and I teach our kids that there are four main principles in the heart of the Declaration:

1. There are absolute truths.
2. Our rights are given to us by God.
3. Government is to be controlled by the people, not the other way around.
4. The pursuit of happiness means you should be able to freely participate in a free market.

You can also have your kids memorize the 56 signers of the Declaration. While it may seem like trivial information, it teaches them to honor sacrifice and to remember that freedom is not free. We have listed the Signers in Appendix B along with the complete Declaration of Independence.

Just remember that the investment of freedom principles you make in your children or grandchildren is an investment that produces results for generations to come. The return on investment will be felt by all future Americans.

WE'RE IN THIS TOGETHER

Thank you for reading our family story, or at least the chapters lived so far! Whether you write to us about what your family is doing to fulfill God's purpose in your lives or we meet one day in person, we hope to hear your family story as well.

Our families are inseparably linked by our common bond as Americans. What you do in your home and community has an impact on our home and community and vice versa.

Each and every one of us has a role to play during this short window of opportunity in which we live our freedom and stand guard at the watchtower of freedom. As we do so, let us purposefully prepare the next generation to do the same.

Lord Willing, the legacy of our generation will be one in which they say that on our watch, the Torch of Freedom burned even brighter than it ever had before!

APPENDIX A

WHAT I SAW AT PRESIDENT
RONALD REAGAN'S FUNERAL

5/10/04 – I'm on the plane flying home from DC, trying to mentally digest the last 24 hours. Dad and I were able to make this trip together to honor President Reagan and attend his funeral procession. As I made plans to attend, I fully expected everything to go wrong. I assumed dad would be unable to get a flight and I would be unable to extend my trip to the northeast (I was speaking in Lancaster, PA). I just knew the event would be hot, crowded, and impersonal. I assumed we'd end up with major logistical problems such as never finding a parking space or a cab. I was afraid we'd end up so far in the back of the crowd and away from the street that we wouldn't even be able to see the caisson carrying our beloved leader and taking a picture to share with my family would be impossible. With 150,000 expected to attend, we knew there was a chance we would stand in line all night and literally all day and still not get into the Capitol Rotunda to pay our respects.

None of these worst case scenarios mattered to me and nothing was going to keep me from honoring, in whatever way I could, the man whom I consider the epitome of leadership and the embodiment of all that is good about America.

Much to our surprise, not one of the above mentioned problems became reality. It was as if the Lord parted the way at every turn we made. His favor allowed us to be in the right place at the right time for an experience I will never forget and will cherish sharing with my grandchildren and beyond.

It's really quite surreal and very difficult to express in words, so I'll just tell the story as I remember it...

First of all, you've got to understand why I would have been willing to stand in that line for the full 36 hours even if I knew I would be told at the doorway that no one else would be allowed inside. To say that I love and respect Ronald Wilson Reagan is a bit of an understatement. My 2nd son is named Reagan Kyle Green, after the President. My 4th child, much to my delight, was born on February 6, 2003, the 92nd birthday of President Reagan. To top things off, my dog is named Dutch, the nickname given to the President by his father.

My first memory of President Reagan is from the day he was shot in 1981. I was barely nine years old, but the surroundings of our living room and the sight of my mother crying as we watched the breaking news are crystal clear in my mind.

In the fall of 1993, my friends and I had become so tired of the distortions of Reagan's legacy that we decided to do something about it. Clinton/Gore had repeated *"worst economy in 50 years"* and other lies so many times that the public was buying into the revision of history. Along with two of my friends from College Republicans, and the man who would later work at my side in the Legislature, Greg Tolen, I produced *"The Legacy of President Ronald Reagan: The Truth About the Eighties"* and also put together a compilation of his greatest speeches. As part of the project, we went to Washington, DC to interview Dick Cheney and Trent Lott. While there, we attended President Reagan's birthday gala. It turned out to be the very last public speech he would give and I was able to meet him for a very brief moment backstage. It was that night that I dedicated myself to becoming a student of freedom and working to preserve it and pass it on to future generations.

Now back to our story... Dad was with me at that dinner in 1994 and here we were, a decade later, making our way to the Capitol to see President Reagan again.

A friend, who happens to be a Congressman, offered to take me in with his sons to the private ceremonies at which Vice-President Cheney was speaking in the Rotunda. But since they were only allowed to bring family, we figured my dad would never pass for his son like I would. I knew I could watch the ceremony on TV when I got back home...but I would never have the chance to experience this day with my father again, so my decision was easy.

Dad was unable to book a flight that would land any earlier at BWI than 4:30, so we assumed we would miss the 6:00 PM processional wherein President Reagan's body would be carried down Constitution Avenue on the horse drawn carriage. Just in case, dad got to the airport at 5:30 AM and was able to fly standby and arrive at BWI at Noon, which changed everything for us.

I picked dad up in my rental car and we started talking about how hot it was going to be and what to wear. Those of you that know me know that you will not catch me in a coat or tie unless it is an absolute must and we were about to be in 95 degree weather for at least 7 hours and possible for two full days. But we kept thinking about President Reagan not taking his jacket off in the Oval Office and decided that we'd sweat this one out for the Gipper (there's nothing in the folk lore about a tie, so you can bet the jacket was my limit!).

We arrived in DC pretty early and decided to park as close to the new WWII Memorial as possible so we could see it on our trip. I wanted to take pictures of specific sections of the memorial to take back to two of my

heroes, Bill Johnson and Jim Roddie of Wimberley, Texas. Knowing that more than 100,000 people were descending on this area in the next couple of hours, I assumed there would be no parking spot in sight. But I also had heard that the Metro would not be running after midnight, so we really didn't have a choice. Much to our surprise, we drove maybe two blocks past the monument and found a perfect parking spot.

We toured the monument and many tears and two rolls of film later, starting making our trek to the Capitol. I thought the staging area for the transfer of President Reagan from the hearse to the caisson was on the other side of the Capitol (a full 30 blocks from where we were), but as we were walking up Constitution, we ran into a ton of metro cars and found that we were right at the staging area and it was about 3:00 PM.

Three hours from now, there would be tens of thousands in this very spot to watch the transfer and the beginning of the procession, but as we looked around, there were very, very few people and we could pick virtually any spot we wanted and be in the very front row. We had to decide whether to take a spot here or move on closer to the Capitol so that we could immediately get in line for the viewing after the procession (we were still 16 blocks, over a mile and a half, from the Capitol). We opted to keep moving.

As we walked up Constitution, tracing the very route President Reagan's casket would take in a few hours, people were sporadically beginning to take places along the road. We kept going until we got to the corner of the Capitol grounds where Pennsylvania and Constitution converge. The line for the viewing had begun early that morning and was right around the corner, so we knew we could go right to the line after the procession.

We picked a spot where there was a bend in the road so our view of the procession was unimpeded by those standing next to us and we literally stood on the front row, right next to the barricade.

The two and a half hour "wait" flew by. On our left was a 12 year old girl named Megan and her mother, Karey. They had flown all night long on Tuesday night from Oregon, arriving in DC at 7:00 AM without sleep. Megan had just written a paper and given a speech on President Reagan. This Twelve year old was breaking down President Reagan's 93 years for me into the six major "lives" that he lived from radio to Hollywood to politics.

Above: Rick & Megan at Reagan Funeral.

Below: In 2009, Megan attended Patriot Academy. She is an outstanding young lady who, like other Patriot graduates, gives me real hope for the future!

Absolutely amazing.

I exchanged photographs with other parents who had named their children after President Reagan and we all shared how he had touched our lives and changed the world. An Army veteran on my right told me that he could think of no more important way to be serving his Country at this moment than to be standing on that sidewalk honoring the Commander and Chief that had restored our nation's heart, soul... and backbone.

We were all calling home and getting reports on what was happening around us. Someone said he was just told that we were standing in the very spot between 4th and Pennsylvania where the 21 Fighter Jets would be flying over.

After the transfer had been made from the hearse to the caisson (which we could not see at all and were more than a mile away from), my wife, Kara, called and described it to me over the phone. They were still a mile away, but the tears already started and the magnitude of the moment began to hit me.

As the procession approached, the crowd became completely silent. Once the first band had passed, all you could hear were camera clicks and the soldiers marching. Each service was represented and it was an awesome, awesome site to see. Such a massive military presence was a fitting tribute for the man that respected and honored them more than any since Eisenhower and for whom there was a mutual level of respect between him and those in uniform.

Following the military was the motorcade leading the caisson. As the motorcade  passed, you could see the flag draped coffin atop the caisson as the horses rounded the corner. What had been near silence seemed to grow even more hushed as the atmosphere transformed from one of anticipation to something I can only describe as surreal.

As the caisson approached us, the moment was forever powerfully etched into each of  us as the silence was broken by the roar of the first jet flying overheard. Twenty more jets flew over us in groups of four. The final group screamed by and a wingman broke away and rocketed upward to signify the loss of a comrade. The last group went overhead literally at the very moment the men leading the caisson reached the point where we stood.

To be anywhere near this procession was powerful by itself. To have the jets fly directly overhead at the very moment President Reagan's coffin was reaching us is an experience impossible to describe with words.

With tears running down my face, I was trying to keep my hand over my heart while also taking pictures for my children to share this moment in years to come. My father was like a statue next to me... standing at erect attention with his hand over his heart. Somehow, I think we had the same thoughts as most everyone around us.

Our memories of President Reagan raced through our minds, as we tried to measure the impact of this man, now reduced to dust as we all will be someday. My first thoughts were how he had impacted me personally. While producing the documentaries, the words of his speeches became imbedded in my mind and a passion for this nation was ignited in my heart. I kept hearing the final words of his 1981 inaugural speech. After extolling the virtues of America and the importance of tackling the issues we faced, he challenged us to *"believe in ourselves"* and *"believe that together, with God's help, we can and will resolve the problems which now confront us."* He closed with the timing of his words as only he could deliver by saying *"...after all, why shouldn't we believe that? We... are Americans."*

With President Reagan, it was always "we" and hardly ever "I." The man that passed before me was best summed up and most honored with exactly the same description he honored and inspired each of us twenty-three years ago. He... was an American.

The most powerful site to me was the empty horse with President Reagan's actual boots backwards in the stirrups. It was a site that would send chills up any spine.

As the caisson continued making its way past us and out of sight, I began to realize that even as momentous as this ceremony was, it barely touched the surface of measuring the impact of this great man. Around me were members of the WWII generation, my parent's generation, my own, and then there was little Megan, all of twelve years old. Not even born when he left office, barely two when he gave that very last public speech in 1994, here she stood as living proof that President Reagan's impact would be felt for many generations to come.

Nancy Reagan's car approached and she waived out the window to all of us. Though it had been probably twenty minutes of continual procession passing before us, the ceremony seemed to suddenly disappear.

APPENDIX A

We made our way to the line, preparing to wait three hours before it would even begin to move as the first of the public would enter the Rotunda. The line was positioned directly in front of the West steps, though at a considerable distance. We were able to watch as the Honor Guard carried the casket up the 99 steps and we could even see Ms. Reagan at the top of the steps.

Once the entire procession was inside the Capitol, we began what would turn out to be a five hour tribute as we made our way through the line to the Rotunda. Somehow the line continued to move forward, even during the hours prior to the person first in line entering the Capitol. We met people from around the country. Everyone was polite, even sharing their snacks and passing out bottles of water. Little Miss Megan gave interviews to television reporters from around the world. No one complained or questioned as people slipped out of line for restroom stops and slipped back into their original places.

Five hours later, as we passed through the last security checkpoint and made our way up the ramps to the Capitol entrance, I thought of how I wished my wife and children could be with me. At the same time, I was both comforted and honored that I would be standing there with the man who had first instilled in me a respect for the things I would grow to love about President Reagan.

As we entered the Capitol, we were warmly greeted by a highly decorated member of the Capitol Police. He was so genuine as he thanked us for attending and we thanked him for his service.

We made our way up the steps inside the Capitol and as we approached the entrance to the Rotunda, we could hear the echoes of steps being taken. Every sound reverberated throughout the room. There  was an obvious desire on everyone's part to linger as a long as possible, but our pauses in front of the casket were brief. A few steps in front of me, a marine in plain clothes stopped for a formal salute. A few steps behind me, a naval officer in full dress uniform did the same. The Honor Guard stationed around the casket was a magnificent sight that I will never forget.

We were handed an embossed card memorializing the ceremony, a treasure for my family for generations to come. We made our way outside and to the street, struggling to let the moment register in our hearts and minds.

We were physically and emotionally exhausted and had a two mile walk to where our rental car would hopefully still be parked. Megan and her mother had no way to get to their hotel as the metro was about to shut down and neither of them had slept in twenty-four hours. Proving chivalry is not dead for Texans, dad waited with them on a bench and I started the hike to the car. Before I could get one block, in what could only be an answer to prayer, a taxi approached from out of nowhere and I had a ride to our car, which was still where we had left it.

We took Megan and her mother to their hotel, found our own, and got a few hours sleep before I did an early morning radio interview and left for the airport. Not one of my concerns had come to pass, yet everything I could have hoped for in the trip had occurred.

If one were to say it was hero worship for so many of us to go to such lengths to watch a casket go by, or to walk by it in the rotunda, they would clearly miss the point. In many ways, this had nothing to do with seeing the procession or approaching the casket. I believe most of us would have done all of this if only to walk by a picture of Reagan or anything that symbolized his contribution to our Nation. In other words, it was not about getting to see or touch or experience anything nearly as much as it was about doing something, though something small, to simply honor him and everything he represented. It was the idea of putting our lives on hold for a couple of days, inconvenient as it may have been, to pay our respects. For hundreds of thousands to do so this week is a small indication of the impact made by the man we honored.

I pray the words and images of this week not only remind us of all that President Reagan accomplished, but also inspire us to pick up where he left off... to accept that torch of freedom he so ably guarded and passed to our generation. There was a common theme to be found in the faces of so many young people that I passed in the lines as we weaved our way back and forth towards the Capitol for five hours. You could see the determination, the inspiration, the desire to be a part of the next wave of the Reagan Revolution.

I could once again hear President Reagan's words from that first inaugural: *"Well, I believe we, the Americans of today, are ready to act worthy of ourselves, ready to do what must be done to ensure happiness and liberty for ourselves, our children and our children's children."*

To those of you who were a part of the Reagan Revolution and have been concerned about whether or not my generation would carry on, I would simply ask that you believe in us as you did in President Reagan. After all, why shouldn't you believe...

WE... ARE AMERICANS!

APPENDIX B

The Declaration of Independence

IN CONGRESS, July 4, 1776.

The unanimous Declaration of the thirteen united States of America,

When in the Course of human events, it becomes necessary for one people to dissolve the political bands which have connected them with another, and to assume among the powers of the earth, the separate and equal station to which the Laws of Nature and of Nature's God entitle them, a decent respect to the opinions of mankind requires that they should declare the causes which impel them to the separation.

We hold these truths to be self-evident, that all men are created equal, that they are endowed by their Creator with certain unalienable Rights, that among these are Life, Liberty and the pursuit of Happiness. That to secure these rights, Governments are instituted among Men, deriving their just powers from the consent of the governed, -- That whenever any Form of Government becomes destructive of these ends, it is the Right of the People to alter or to abolish it, and to institute new Government, laying its foundation on such principles and organizing its powers in such form, as to them shall seem most likely to effect their Safety and Happiness. Prudence, indeed, will dictate that Governments long established should not be changed for light and transient causes; and accordingly all experience hath shewn, that mankind are more disposed to suffer, while evils are sufferable, than to right themselves by abolishing the forms to which they are accustomed. But when a long train of abuses and usurpations, pursuing invariably the same Object evinces a design to reduce them under absolute Despotism, it is their right, it is their duty, to throw off such Government, and to provide new Guards for their future security.--Such has been the patient sufferance of these Colonies; and such is now the necessity which constrains them to alter their former Systems of Government. The history of the present King of Great Britain is a history of repeated injuries and usurpations, all having in direct object the establishment of an absolute Tyranny over these States. To prove this, let Facts be submitted to a candid world.

He has refused his Assent to Laws, the most wholesome and necessary for the public good.

He has forbidden his Governors to pass Laws of immediate and pressing importance, unless suspended in their operation till his Assent should be obtained; and when so suspended, he has utterly neglected to attend to them.

He has refused to pass other Laws for the accommodation of large districts of people, unless those people would relinquish the right of Representation in the Legislature, a right inestimable to them and formidable to tyrants only.

He has called together legislative bodies at places unusual, uncomfortable, and distant from the depository of their public Records, for the sole purpose of fatiguing them into compliance with his measures.

He has dissolved Representative Houses repeatedly, for opposing with manly firmness his invasions on the rights of the people.

He has refused for a long time, after such dissolutions, to cause others to be elected; whereby the Legislative powers, incapable of Annihilation, have returned to the People at large for their exercise; the State remaining in the mean time exposed to all the dangers of invasion from without, and convulsions within.

He has endeavored to prevent the population of these States; for that purpose obstructing the Laws for Naturalization of Foreigners; refusing to pass others to encourage their migrations hither, and raising the conditions of new Appropriations of Lands.

He has obstructed the Administration of Justice, by refusing his Assent to Laws for establishing Judiciary powers.

He has made Judges dependent on his Will alone, for the tenure of their offices, and the amount and payment of their salaries.

He has erected a multitude of New Offices, and sent hither swarms of Officers to harass our people, and eat out their substance.

He has kept among us, in times of peace, Standing Armies without the Consent of our legislatures.

He has affected to render the Military independent of and superior to the Civil Power.

He has combined with others to subject us to a jurisdiction foreign to our constitution, and unacknowledged by our laws; giving his Assent to their Acts of pretended Legislation:

For quartering large bodies of armed troops among us:

For protecting them, by a mock Trial, from punishment for any Murders which they should commit on the Inhabitants of these States:

For cutting off our Trade with all parts of the world:

For imposing Taxes on us without our Consent:

For depriving us in many cases, of the benefits of Trial by Jury:

For transporting us beyond Seas to be tried for pretended offences

For abolishing the free System of English Laws in a neighboring Province, establishing therein an Arbitrary government, and enlarging its Boundaries so as to render it at once an example and fit instrument for introducing the same absolute rule into these Colonies:

For taking away our Charters, abolishing our most valuable Laws, and altering fundamentally the Forms of our Governments:

For suspending our own Legislatures, and declaring themselves invested with power to legislate for us in all cases whatsoever.

He has abdicated Government here, by declaring us out of his Protection and waging War against us.

He has plundered our seas, ravaged our Coasts, burnt our towns, and destroyed the lives of our people.

He is at this time transporting large Armies of foreign Mercenaries to complete the works of death, desolation and tyranny, already begun with circumstances of Cruelty & perfidy scarcely paralleled in the most barbarous ages, and totally unworthy the Head of a civilized nation.

He has constrained our fellow Citizens taken Captive on the high Seas to bear Arms against their Country, to become the executioners of their friends and Brethren, or to fall themselves by their Hands.

He has excited domestic insurrections amongst us, and has endeavored to bring on the inhabitants of our frontiers, the merciless Indian Savages, whose known rule of warfare, is an undistinguished destruction of all ages, sexes and conditions.

In every stage of these Oppressions We have Petitioned for Redress in the most humble terms: Our repeated Petitions have been answered only by repeated injury. A Prince whose character is thus marked by every act which may define a Tyrant, is unfit to be the ruler of a free people.

Nor have We been wanting in attentions to our British brethren. We have warned them from time to time of attempts by their legislature to extend an unwarrantable jurisdiction over us. We have reminded them of the circumstances of our emigration and settlement here. We have appealed to their native justice and magnanimity, and we have conjured them by the ties of our common kindred to disavow these usurpations, which, would inevitably interrupt our connections and correspondence. They too have been deaf to the voice of justice and of consanguinity. We must, therefore, acquiesce in the necessity, which denounces our Separation, and hold them, as we hold the rest of mankind, Enemies in War, in Peace Friends.

We, therefore, the Representatives of the united States of America, in General Congress, Assembled, appealing to the Supreme Judge of the world for the rectitude of our intentions, do, in the Name, and by Authority of the good People of these Colonies, solemnly publish and declare, That these United Colonies are, and of Right ought to be Free and Independent States;

that they are Absolved from all Allegiance to the British Crown, and that all political connection between them and the State of Great Britain, is and ought to be totally dissolved; and that as Free and Independent States, they have full Power to levy War, conclude Peace, contract Alliances, establish Commerce, and to do all other Acts and Things which Independent States may of right do. And for the support of this Declaration, with a firm reliance on the protection of divine Providence, we mutually pledge to each other our Lives, our Fortunes and our sacred Honor.

The 56 signatures on the Declaration

Connecticut:
Roger Sherman
Samuel Huntington
William Williams
Oliver Wolcott

Delaware:
Caesar Rodney
George Read
Thomas McKean

Georgia:
Button Gwinnett
Lyman Hall
George Walton

Maryland:
Samuel Chase
William Paca
Thomas Stone
Charles Carroll

South Carolina:
Edward Rutledge
Thomas Heyward, Jr.
Thomas Lynch, Jr.
Arthur Middleton

New Hampshire:
Josiah Bartlett
William Whipple
Matthew Thornton

New Jersey:
Richard Stockton
John Witherspoon
Francis Hopkinson
John Hart
Abraham Clark

New York:
William Floyd
Philip Livingston
Francis Lewis
Lewis Morris

North Carolina:
William Hooper
Joseph Hewes
John Penn

Rhode Island:
Stephen Hopkins
William Ellery

Virginia:
George Wythe
Richard Henry Lee
Thomas Jefferson
Benjamin Harrison
Thomas Nelson, Jr.
Francis Lightfoot Lee
Carter Braxton

Massachusetts:
Samuel Adams
John Adams
John Hancock
Robert Treat Paine
Elbridge Gerry

Pennsylvania:
Robert Morris
Benjamin Rush
Benjamin Franklin
John Morton
George Clymer
James Smith
George Taylor
James Wilson
George Ross

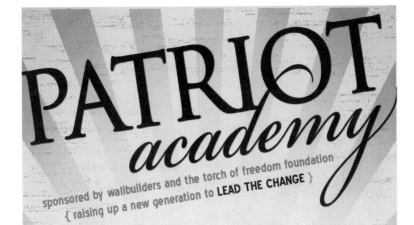

PATRIOT *academy*

sponsored by wallbuilders and the torch of freedom foundation
{ raising up a new generation to **LEAD THE CHANGE** }

CHALLENGE YOUR IDEA OF GOVERNMENT

At Patriot Academy, you don't just learn about government, you live it. This summer, you and your fellow students, ages 16-25, will take over the Texas state government at the Capitol Building in Austin, Texas. You will work together to form a fully functioning mock government, drafting legislation, running committee meetings, debating bills, electing leaders and passing laws.

CONFRONT THE ISSUES OF TODAY

In a fast-paced, interactive format, elected officials and experts will explain today's most relevant issues. Through media relations training, public speaking workshops and spirited debate, you will learn to articulate what you believe and why. Patriot Academy will equip you to effect change for the issues that matter most to you, whether as a concerned citizen or political candidate.

CHAMPION THE CAUSE OF FREEDOM

If you want to be a part of a new generation of young leaders poised to change the future of American politics, join us at Patriot Academy. You won't want to miss it!

To order more of Rick & Kara Green's products,
go to **www.rickgreen.com**

Is America One Nation Under God?
In Rick's most popular presentation, we
discover whether or not our nation was
founded on biblical principles
Available on DVD, audio CD, & booklet

The Birth of Freedom
Journey back before 1776, when the first seeds of
freedom were planted, to learn about the
Revolutionary Strategies of the Founding Fathers.
You will also hear about America's first War on
Radical Islamic Terrorism & how our first 4
presidents won the same fight America now faces
Available on DVD & audio CD

The Guardian of Liberty
Rick defends the "Pursuit of Happiness" through
our free competitive enterprise system, and
makes the case for choosing only leaders who
have faith in the free market
Available on DVD & audio CD

Collection of Historical Presentations
This set includes a DVD & audio CD of Rick's
following presentations: Is America One
Nation Under God, The Birth of Freedom, The
Guardian of Liberty

Saving America Begins With You!

Have America's best days come & gone? No, but if she is to be saved, it must begin with you! Rick lays out a realistic blueprint for how American Values can defeat the policies threatening us today

Available on DVD & audio CD

The Legacy of Ronald Reagan

This DVD documentary sets the record straight to show the dynamic accomplishments made during the Presidency of Ronald Reagan

Available on DVD

Freedom's Frame

This book covers in depth the founding principles behind America's success and action steps for preserving freedom.

Available on audio CD or paperback book

Our American Story

This book is also available on audio CD